TRULY ASKEW

TRULY ASKEW

Alistair McHarg

2018

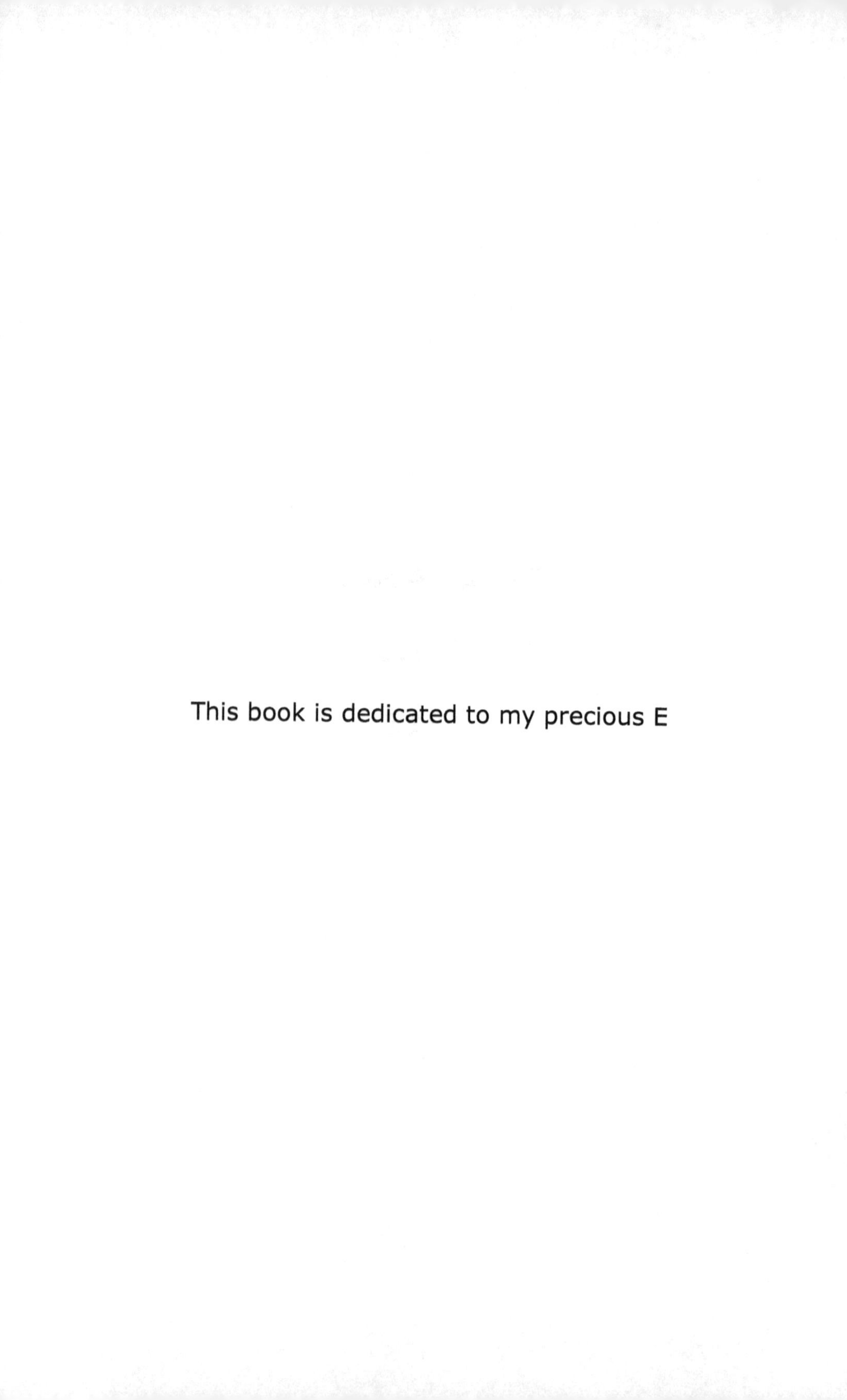

This book is dedicated to my precious E

"The absurd is the essential concept and the first truth."

Albert Camus

CONTENTS

QUOTES BY TOPIC

INTRODUCTION

Reality is absurd. Impossible. Ludicrous. Despite this, humanity labors tirelessly in a misguided attempt to make sense of it. The folly of this enterprise grows ever more apparent as one attempts to crack the cosmic code; knowing more leads inevitably to understanding less.

Embracing the chaotic irrationality of existence, and taking delight in it, is preferable to being disappointed, even enraged, by the mystery. Learning to view preposterousness not as an enemy but an ally offers enormous advantages to those keen on enjoying life.

The level of acceptance required to accomplish this did not come naturally to me. At the advanced age of 36, fate unceremoniously dumped me on the path of spiritual growth, slammed the door, and locked it. The demon in charge of my education was Manic Depression (Bipolar Disorder).

Mania raged in the full flower of its righteous, unhinged glory; complete with random strikes of lightning and unrepentant wrath. Pieces of my bourgeois life fled magically; marriage, house, money, jobs, even family. Racing recklessly around a yawning void, I finally summoned the courage to fight.

With determination born of terror, desperation, and more than a little spite, I plunged headfirst into talk therapy. There was no other option. Defeating one of the most severe forms of mental illness demanded a search for the source of my fears. I embarked on an internal odyssey.

To fully understand what had happened, and to help others as well, I wrote a memoir about my experience (*Invisible Driving*). This proved to be a fantastically difficult undertaking, both technically and emotionally. Upon completion, I bathed for some time in the illusion of mastery. I thought my struggles were done.

Complacency brought a different internal monster to the foreground: addiction. After plowing my car into a cement barricade, fate slammed yet another door and ushered me into the nicotine-stained church basements of Alcoholics Anonymous.

In AA I found camaraderie, discipline, and practical philosophy. Having been "softened up" by many years of therapy, I absorbed ideas quickly and was soon regarded as a de facto teacher. While I had assiduously avoided this role all my life, I learned to love it simply because, for the first time, I was well positioned to be of service.

That was 18 clean and sober years ago (I even gave up cigarettes). The spiritual path led me to the point where I avoid self-destructive behavior in favor of health and usefulness. Being a writer, this naturally led to sharing my experience publicly; hence, *Truly Askew*.

Buried within the ramshackle humor, tactless sincerity, and unrepentant iconoclasm of these 72 vignettes and 240 quotes, is a thoroughly authentic story of recovery and redemption I hope will delight, amuse, reveal, and provoke.

All stories and essays were originally written individually and assembled chronologically later. Some are autobiographical snapshots, some dive into the experience of bipolar disorder and substance abuse, while others speak directly to the recovery process. There are even a few satirical sketches which first appeared in my mental health humor column.

Interspersed are epigrams, adages, and aphorisms. These enigmatic tidbits have an amusing genesis. About ten years ago I began noticing the deplorable abuse of quotes on the Internet. Each new day brought wave after wave of mangled, misinterpreted, and often inaccurately attributed quotes.

As a lark, I began cranking out gassy, nonsensical quips oozing faux gravitas and attributed them to the silliest name I could imagine: Taz Mopula. No one called my bluff; on the contrary, Taz Mopulisms grew in popularity. Today you will find them scattered far and wide, resting cheek by jowl with thought nuggets by the likes of Wilde, Twain, and Einstein.

But the joke was on me, I'm afraid. What began as performance art morphed into a passion bordering on obsession. Over the years I have created, illustrated, and curated 100s and 100s of these sayings, and no longer hide behind the Taz Mopula pseudonym. For *Truly Askew* I winnowed my collection down as far as I could and grouped the survivors by topic.

The quotes are united by my quest for immutable truth. Many are absurd, self-contradictory, funny, odd, counterintuitive, maddening, and uncooperative in a host of other ways. I did not set out to make them difficult, they are truly askew because life is truly askew. Frankly, the true of life is often most evident in the askew-ness of it.

The vignettes guide you along my journey of discovery; the quotes glow with the insight and happiness that came of it.

Alistair McHarg
Sandown, New Hampshire
April 2018

ADVENTURE

Sometimes you must leave home to find your way home.

If you don't know where you're going you can never be lost.

One's horizon can never be too broad, one's crew can never be too valiant, and one's ocean can never be too wet.

Portrait of The Artist as A Short Man

By the time I arrived in Philadelphia at age six I had already lived in three different countries and learned two very different languages. My writerly personality – detached, solitary, depressed, thoughtful, lonely, mercurial, disingenuous, acquiescent, analytical, misanthropic, and insecure – was already well in place. Drug abuse, chronic isolation, and a rich assortment of self-destructive behaviors lurked just around the bend.

I once asked a professor what it took to make a living as a writer. Without pausing he said, "You have to give up any hope of leading a normal life." When I asked him that question I thought I had a choice, I did not understand that the decision had already been made for me.

I was a serious wee lad, a miniature adult; the world was too much upon me. By six I was already scribbling poetry about God, death, and the meaning of life. Time allowed me to grow up, or down, into my image of an aspiring, young artist – miraculously I never owned a beret, probably because I do not wear hats well. I pursued sensual indulgence, cheap thrills, and bourgeois decadence with relish.

I enjoyed the feeling of squandering talent, wasting opportunities, and pissing away gifts others might have killed to enjoy. It was an era of bad boys and anti-heroes and although I did indeed turn bad it never made me a hero. Also, somewhere along the way I stopped writing anything more culturally consequential than foot powder ads.

It was only through traversing the burning landscapes of manic depression (bipolar disorder) that I was forced to break my personality down into its most primary elements and reconstruct. That process, hard as it was, gave me so many glorious gifts, among them the ability to have fun and play.

I read once that it is never too late to have a happy childhood – and I have taken that as my mantra. As far as I am concerned – He who dies having had the most fun, wins. I learned at last that having fun is not difficult, complex, or costly – it is simply a matter of knowing yourself, being yourself, and enjoying being yourself.

There is a coda to this song. You allow other people to enjoy you enjoying being yourself, too.

ADVICE

It is unwise to purchase a dog more interesting than you are.

If I could only give you one piece of advice it would be this: Do not, under any circumstances, take my advice.

Giving advice exquisitely pairs the illusion of generosity with serene unaccountability; since no one ever takes it.

Imprisoned Apes Escape into Addiction

When I was a very young lad living in Edinburgh, I would go on perambulations with my mother. Edinburgh is a grand city for walking, and we explored it at length. (As a Dutch woman recently transplanted from Amsterdam I think she found it as exotic as I did.) Edinburgh Castle, with its steep, cobblestone ascent, was a favorite haunt. I also loved the expansive train station, spewing steam as if the arched glass roof concealed a nest of restless dragons. And then there was the zoo.

It was at the Edinburgh Zoo that I rode my first elephant; and one never forgets one's first elephant ride; nor, for that matter, do they. There was no shortage of star attractions, but by far the most popular was Charlie the Gorilla, so named in honor of Bonnie Prince Charlie. Charlie was a 400-pound, silverback gorilla from the Congo. Even as a small child I was moved by his soulful face, power, and imprisonment. But crowds did not gather to marvel at his size and strength; they came to see him smoke.

In post-war Scotland, cigarettes were a scarce, expensive luxury. Despite this, working class visitors tossed lit cigarettes into the cage for Charlie to enjoy, and he did so with panache, carefully secreting them behind his back when his keeper arrived. (This Heckle and Jeckle routine had been polished smooth as a vaudeville act. Charlie exhaled clouds of smoke flamboyantly, exhibiting satisfaction Bob Marley might have envied. Then, when his keeper looked over, the cigarette vanished into one of his massive, furry hands. The routine never got old, and when the keeper knitted his eyebrows in disapproval, the kids howled with delight.)

In those days my parents were barely scraping by, even so, cigarettes were a line item in the family budget. My mother did not smoke but my father bought them every day in packs of 5. Later on, in more prosperous times, he smoked the way waitresses chew gum, obsessively, constantly, thoughtlessly.

As a youth I quickly came to understand that smoking was something cool people did, and I was physically and psychologically addicted well before leaving high school. Cigarettes were my one, true friend through it all. I smoked in prison and in mental hospitals, on the desolate streets of North Philadelphia at midnight; I even smoked at The White House.

Over time, unceremonious, bare-knuckle education pushed the rogue's gallery of vices beyond my grasp, as a ship gradually drifts away from the dock. Alcohol and drugs, abandoned almost two decades ago, now seem foreign and counter-productive. But smoking clung to me like a tick, it was the very last to leave. In the waning days of squandering a fortune on this bizarre activity it became, at last, like a vestigial tribute to a life of self-destruction.

I'd like to go back to Edinburgh and tell Charlie, "You're a 400-pound silverback gorilla from the Congo. You're fabulous. You don't need cigarettes to be cool. You're already pretty damn cool."

ANTI-SOCIAL NETWORKING

It doesn't qualify as listening if you're busy thinking what to say next.

Today the average attention span is barely long enough to reach from one end of a sentence to the...squirrel!

Help eliminate communication pollution. If you have nothing of value to say, say it only as often as absolutely necessary.

Our ability to broadcast the wretched detritus of daily life is no argument for doing so; restraint is increasingly precious.

The Main Thing WWII Taught My Dad

My father was a gifted storyteller. If I was good he would tell me one at bedtime. My favorite concerned a troop ship anchored in the Mediterranean, off the coast of Italy. This is how it went.

He and his men were asleep; it was late at night and silent. (My dad fought through the entirety of WWII, he was a Major in the British Army and commanded the 2nd Parachute Squadron of Royal Engineers.) Suddenly they were awakened by a horrific explosion that caused the ship to burst into flames, throwing shrapnel in every direction.

He painted a picture of the madness in glowing detail, terrified men racing to get on deck before the ship sank, men torn open by flying bits of debris, screaming men whose clothes were ablaze, men leaping overboard into the cold water.

He described jumping into the sea and watching as the ship became engulfed in red, yellow, orange, blue, black, and white until, in short minutes, everyone on it was dead. Then, he turned his gaze to the dark water around him, looking for anything he could use to stay afloat. Doing so he noticed a fellow soldier flailing his arms wildly and screaming for help. My dad swam over to the poor wretch and gripped his collar.

But – (my dad always slowed down for this part and went sotto voce) – what he hadn't counted on was that the man did not know how to swim and was in a state of irrational, hysterical fear. Madly, desperately, the man grabbed onto my father as if he were mere flotsam, and in so doing began pulling the both of them, by now entwined like doomed serpents, below the water.

At this point, my dad confessed, it was his turn to panic. He understood there was no saving this man and attempting to do so would simply bump the body count from one to two. He detailed the complex moral soul searching that occurred in mere seconds before he bit the man's fingers to break the death grip, finally separating the two of them. A few strong kicks pushed him safely away and he watched the man's hands churn water until at last he fell to the depths of the Mediterranean Sea and into an unmarked grave.

Then my dad would gently brush the hair off my forehead and whisper, "The best way to help the dead is by not being one of them."

ARROGANCE

Arrogance: What stupidity wants to be when it grows up.

Arrogance and wisdom cannot coexist; the more you learn, the less important you become.

Arrogance and intelligence are well-acquainted, but arrogance and wisdom are strangers.

While many insist on making it a group activity, being right can also be enjoyed without companionship.

It Isn't the Caboose That Kills You

Even as a kid I had difficulty managing money. Along with my sketchy friends I'd go to the nearby abandoned coal yard and lay pennies out on the railroad tracks, collecting what remained once the trains were gone. If you've ever done this yourself you know that Lincoln is no longer recognizable, what's left looks like a frozen, wafer-thin copper puddle.

Dancing on and off the tracks, putting our ears against the rails to gauge how far away the trains were; this was all part of the illicit fun. We were young and immortal, mindless to risk.

My parents were immigrants and loved this country in a way unique to immigrants – awed by the scale and opportunity. They liked to tell me about a trip out west they took as newlyweds. Picnic spread across an Indian blanket, vast expanse of desert splayed out before them, they watched an endless freight train snaking past. On a whim they decided to count the boxcars.

Revealing the number dramatically, as if I hadn't heard the story a dozen times before, my mother would report, "Two-hundred-and-twenty-eight cars from engines to caboose," with awe she might have just as easily applied to a description of the Grand Canyon or her first time up The Empire State Building.

The vast wealth and immensity of their adopted nation lay in stunning contrast to the post-war Holland my mother had left, and my father's native Scotland, not especially prosperous even In the best of times.

One of the particularly American habits my parents adopted in their zeal to be real U.S. citizens was drinking martinis. I can see them now, on the patio behind the kitchen, my father pouring from a stainless-steel shaker into glasses reserved for these occasions. They each had two, always with a twist of lemon peel.

If they were feeling especially jolly, my father would carefully strain out what was left at the bottom, mingled in with the melting ice. This was enough for half a martini each, which my father referred to as – "the Dean's half" – in honor of Sir Peter Shepherd, acting Dean of my father's department at U. of P.

My family tree is thick with accomplishment on both sides, but I am the very first to achieve the title of "alcoholic." Dad was mad as a March hare, workaholic, and manic depressive; but no drunk. He understood on a cellular level something I never did, specifically, martinis are like women's breasts; one isn't enough and three are too many.

And so, when I entered the rooms of AA on my hands and knees, utterly defeated, and somebody said, "It isn't the caboose that kills you, man, it's the locomotive," I knew exactly what they meant.

ART

Art is what we have instead of answers.

Art is the shortest distance between two points in cases where one point has no known, or knowable, location.

For admirers, aficionados, critics, and groupies, art is a sacred temple; for actual artists it is a rodeo in the rain.

What Is a Friend?

At sixteen I went on a 1,200-mile canoe trip down the Albany River to Hudson Bay, two months of white water with nine other guys my age, Pete, our group leader, and an Ojibwa Indian guide. Absolute wilderness, our only company the occasional bear or moose. My best friend's name was Terry.

Every evening we set up a new site, cut tent poles and firewood, and cooked dinner. One evening, after a long, exhausting day of paddling in the rain, we found a spot and I went to chop firewood. My axe glanced off a wet tree, through my sock, and deep into my left ankle. (We kept our axes sharp!)

Warm blood soaked my sock; the milky-white anklebone was clearly visible. Pete made me lie down on the ground face up, so he could sew the wound back together using a curved needle, nylon thread, and fishing knots he knew. I was close to passing out. He gave me a piece of wood to bite on, so I wouldn't swallow my tongue and said, "Clamp down hard when it starts hurting."

I looked up and saw a neat circle of faces looking down at me, a combination of sympathy and morbid fascination in their eyes. Everyone was there, except Terry. I felt betrayed, forgotten and let down by my best friend. No one spoke as Pete started sewing and I tried my best not to scream. The only sound was a faint, steady chip chip chip far away.

When they carried me back to my tent, Terry presented me with a beautiful cane he had just carved. Everything I knew, or have come to know, about friendship reverberated in that moment.

AT THE FAIR

If only forgiveness delighted us as intensely as vengeance does.

Religious faith does not prove morality any more than atheism proves intelligence.

The world is most certainly not a fair place, which, for the vast majority of us, is fortunate indeed.

Show Time Is No Time for Mercy

For twelve consecutive years I occupied space in an academic hothouse we'll call St. Frampton Academy, an oasis of genteel entitlement located, improbably, in a Philadelphia neighborhood called Germantown. Germantown was very chic in the horse and carriage days, today it is known for its cobblestone streets, colonial architecture, urban decay, and crime.

All St. Frampton Academy graduates went on to name-brand colleges and universities, universally admired marquee status institutions. This tradition was accepted as law, like gravity, or the idea that everybody likes Italian food. While quality standards were high throughout, St. Frampton Academy was particularly proud of its music department which enjoyed an international reputation. Indeed, its choir would routinely embark on European tours, working rooms like York Minster, widely considered the world's greatest Gothic cathedral.

Presiding over the music department with the subtlety Idi Amin brought to the task of governing Uganda, and standing just five feet tall, Abigail Urqhardt – Miss Urqhardt to us – was built like a fireplug. Childless and single she ate, slept, sneezed, and certainly dreamed music which was no mere career for her but a language with which one could express the ineffable, a transcendent world where miracles were always nearby. A merciless perfectionist she beat us like drums inspiring resentment, fear, admiration, and fierce loyalty.

Miss Urqhardt was fanatical about punctuality and begrudgingly endured an endless succession of excuses for tardiness, often penned by doting parents keen to grease the skids for children already suffering from a surfeit of privilege and indulgence. One day during choir practice a young lady swept into the room late and demonstrated a level of contrition insufficient to satisfy Miss Urqhardt. She froze, scanned the entire room silently, and spoke at last.

"The day will come when you are on stage performing this piece with a room full of people looking right at you. You will be judged on your performance alone. You will not have the opportunity to say to the audience – I'm sorry this performance isn't better but my mom had a flat tire and I got to rehearsal late – I'm sorry my entrances are sloppy but my brother stole my sheet music – I'm sorry that what you're about to hear isn't as good as it could be but I had lacrosse practice. I'm sorry, I'm sorry, I'm sorry."

We looked at the floor, avoiding her eyes. "Excuses," she said at last, "are for ***amateurs***" – practically spitting the final word.

AUDIENCE

An artist can rise no higher than their audience is willing to fly.

The audience is never wrong; that said, one does occasionally wander into the wrong theater.

Even the greatest paintings are flat; they only become three-dimensional in the eyes of those who behold them.

Dismantling the Vatican

My father was beyond judgmental; he was an imperious iconoclast with opinions about absolutely everything. The Professor expressed thoughts in the form of edicts and proclamations, as if to say disagreement was a pointless exercise. One did not have discussions with the old man, much less debates. One was educated.

My family travelled a great deal when I was young, and my dad, an architect and aficionado of aesthetics, among other things, was fond of dragging us to cultural touchstones like cathedrals, gardens, and art galleries. He would explain, with signature irreverence, (much to the horror of passers-by), and we would listen with appropriate respect, if we knew what was good for us.

I remember walking through the Vatican with him. Together we examined every gilt detail of this opulent, overwrought warehouse, admiring the way it oozed wretched excess at once gaudy and operatic, carefully designed to intimidate and lure with meretricious sparkle. Sweeping his arm in grand theatricality he exhaled loudly and sneered, "Cecil B. DeMille."

My father was no mere agnostic, I should point out, but a snarling atheist who put nature in the place frequently occupied by God. Still, he admired cathedrals from an architectural standpoint and an artistic one. He was much taken by the cathedrals in France and made sure to remind us that the men who built them often worked their entire lives without seeing the finished product, indeed, many of these monuments required centuries to complete, and, generations of stone carvers toiled in anonymity, devoting their skill, art, passion, and best energies to a higher calling.

How does the old saw go about the man who plants a tree knowing he will never live to sit in its shade?

BETTER LEFT UNSAID

What you don't see is almost as important as how you don't see it.

Ultimately, it's not what you don't say that matters most so much as how you don't say it.

The Rising Tide of Wretched Detritus

My father had no friends. He had fans, sycophants, students, hostages, admirers, toadies, followers, victims, listeners, and viewers – but no friends. He and my mother did, however, have a select circle of acquaintances. Without exception the men were Type A, driven, and – like my father – leaders in their respective fields. The women were, also without exception, extremely bright, high born, nice, and beautiful.

This "fast set" socialized regularly and their parties were love songs to designer decadence. Alcohol flowed like blood in the streets of Pamplona, as did testosterone. Ego and intellect, style and substance, need for attention and inflated self-image battled it out for supremacy; with the passing of time came increasing volume and hilarity.

As a child I marvelled at these circuses and noticed that my father and male friends always spoke simultaneously; these were not conversations, they were shouting matches. I learned the reason why at his funeral. One of the few remaining lions revealed that, since they had no intention of listening to one another, speaking all at once saved time.

Without paternal guidance, I had to learn what having a friend is all about on my own, and there were many stumbles. For example, narcissism and friendship don't mix. The axiom that goes – to have a friend you must *be* a friend – became meaningful. This, I discovered, involved learning about the needs and wants of other people, and placing them above your own – a strange concept for an alcoholic! And yet, like a thick-headed child, the penny eventually dropped.

Of all the skills required, perhaps the most foreign was listening. I knew about scoring points for talking, even singing; but listening was something very different. Harder still was listening to quiet without feeling an intense need to violate it.

Happily, my Quaker education served me well. Although I am a slave to the savage charms of music, natural orchestras of all descriptions, and the allure of my own voice, I now understand silence to be the only perfect sound.

Tuning out clutter, both external (motorcycles, marching bands, etc.) and internal (ego, fear, anger, etc.), enables me to really listen. Becoming an empty vessel makes it possible to fully witness other people and absorb the eloquent silences.

The irony, of course, is that I find myself in what is commonly referred to as the age of communication – which I think of as the age of digital pollution. Today we are besieged with information and, to pick a number from a hat, about 99% of it is rubbish. While it may not be inherently evil, we are left with the challenge of defending ourselves against the deluge and sifting through what's left on the odd chance of finding something nourishing.

COMMUNICATION

At what point does communication become air pollution?

Why is it called the age of communication when nobody listens?

Instant, universal communication has made it impossible to know if anyone is saying anything valuable.

Manic Depression: Jimi Hendrix

I was just 17 on March 31, 1968, the night I saw Jimi Hendrix perform in a tiny, converted tire warehouse in Philadelphia. Hendrix is iconic today, so I don't need to describe the show. But back then he was absolutely new, unlike anything anyone had ever encountered before. Playing with the guitar behind his head, between his legs, plucking the strings with his teeth – it was astonishing. But most of all it was loud – air raid siren loud. It overwhelmed like an Old Testament rain of fire.

When Hendrix unleashed his signature hit, Manic Depression, I had absolutely no idea what the term meant, much less that it would soon come to define my life. That concert was, perhaps, my first look at mania – real mania – the kind of mania that says – "I am about to set the world ablaze and if you don't like it you better get the fuck out of my way." It was thrilling and overwhelming. We did not suspect he was a meteor, burning up right before our eyes, and that he would be dead in two short years.

Hendrix was certainly not the only musical genius I've seen in concert, but the experience was unique all the same. It is difficult to explain. A year later, in the summer of 1969, I worked for the Bureau of Land Management in Alaska, fighting forest fires. I was part of a back-burning crew, meaning I walked through burning forests carrying a flamethrower. It was like that. A few years later, in Louisville, Kentucky, I watched a tornado tear through the city like hellfire, tossing houses into the air before smashing them to splinters like a fist. It was like that.

The tragedy of Hendrix is that we get to enjoy his work, but he doesn't. He stepped onto the Bipolar Express and never got off, hitting the wall at 100 mph. The poor guy was 27 when he died, with just 4 completed albums to his name.

In the years separating 1968 and 2018 I have come to understand mania only too well, and the music of Jimi Hendrix is encoded in my DNA. One of the many, many reasons I have to be grateful is that fame and adulation did not fuel my illness as they did for Hendrix; I would certainly be dead if they had.

Manic Depression is a frustratin' mess!

CONFUSION

The moment you are certain that you've got it all worked out is precisely when you finally not do.

The realization that something is possible frequently gives rise to the illusion that it is advisable, even necessary.

Righteous Rage in The Sky

On April 4, 1968, my father was returning home from a speaking engagement in Grand Junction, Colorado – connecting with a flight from Denver to Philadelphia. His regular flight had been cancelled and he'd been forced to hop a twin-engine puddle-jumper.

A volatile storm system had parked itself over the continental divide, a two-mile high Rocky Mountain ridge bisecting the state – and the nation – on a North/South axis. The pilots were disinclined to make the trip, especially since my father was the only passenger in their 8-seater. Dad, a former British Army Major and paratrooper, was not easily denied. The three of them ascended.

It wasn't long before the pilot and co-pilot regretted their decision. With only mountains below them, and no available place to land, they pressed on into an increasingly violent, turbulent storm – swimming in rain-whipped blackness, tossed about by sudden shifts of wind, and terrified as lightning strikes grew closer and closer, scarring the dark like heavenly spears.

The pilot and co-pilot were hanging on every word crackling from the radio. My father, anxious to make certain they did their very best, was in the cockpit with them. Then, an urgent voice broke into the control tower feed with the astonishing announcement that Dr. Martin Luther King, Jr. had been assassinated. For an instant the three men, precariously suspended above mountaintops, went silent. At last the pilot spoke. "Finally! They finally took care of that fucking uppity nigger!"

At that moment my father did not think, he acted. Hand out he grabbed the pilot's collar and pulled him forward. Then, fuelled with the irresistible intoxicant we call righteous rage; he punched the pilot full force in the face, knocking him across the cabin. He reached out and repeated the procedure until finally the man, screaming in fear and disbelief, placed both hands on his face to stop the stream of blood pouring from his nose. With authority and conviction that were normal for him my father told the co-pilot to make do without his partner and walked to the back of the small, trembling plane.

There is something wonderfully insane about an individual who would mercilessly beat a man whose well-being was instrumental to continued life, based only on moral outrage. There is also something wildly ironic about defending the memory of a pacifist icon with brute violence. I confess, like Dr. King, I believe passionately in pacifism. And yet, dear reader, there are moments when I ache to be that person, the brute my father was, raining divine retribution on sinners with terrible, swift justice.

Even today I miss Dr. King. Not just for what he did, but especially how he did it. It is the how of it that holds the greatest nobility.

CONTEMPLATION

Think twice before burning bridges; you never know when you might want to jump off one of them.

We are all equal. Those who recognize this, believe it, and incorporate it into their daily lives, are superior; therefore, unequal.

The inability to pay attention erases all advantages gained by intelligence, education, and oh my goodness, look at the time.

Killer in The Dining Room

Moonlit Tours, my debut novel, is a dark comedy exploring the fundamental question – are human beings intrinsically good and evil – or – is evil behavior the consequence of increasingly questionable choices? There are many interwoven storylines involving incremental falls from grace, where essentially decent people find themselves committing unspeakable acts – including murder.

As a young man I was spared the experience of military service and have seen little of death, much less murder. So, when I was preparing to write I scoured my memory for interactions with killers. The most useful was an uncomfortable familiarity with convicted murderer Ira Einhorn, whose unapologetic expression stared out from front pages across the nation some time back. This is the story of how I came to know him.

People rarely rise to the pinnacle of their profession by accident; usually they are driven by a primal force like greed, competitiveness, or the need for approval. My father, who lived his entire life in a state of hypo-mania, genuinely loved what he did; but the emotional engine powering him was an almost pathological need for validation and respect.

I have no first-hand acquaintance with celebrity, but I learned a great deal about it growing up in his shadow. One of the first things I found out is that stars attract sycophants; while some crave only the warmth of reflected limelight, others seek to attach themselves for manipulative, unsavoury purposes. Luminaries, because they are accustomed to praise and crave it like morphine; are easily victimized by the latter variety. Meet Ira Einhorn.

Ira Einhorn was a self-styled anti-war, environmental activist who collaborated with Jerry Rubin and Abbie Hoffman. As the first Earth Day approached, he launched an intense lobbying effort to get on my father's good side, so he could claim some of the credit for organizing it.

I remember him sitting at the massive Nakashima dining table in our house, overlooking Fairmount Park, schmoozing with desperate relentlessness, and my father, clueless as only the truly brilliant can be, falling for it with a broad smile. Einhorn was smart, charming, affable, and determined. He had an unerring instinct for isolating what made people tick and putting it to his advantage.

Earth Day took place in 1970. In 1977 we learned that Einhorn had murdered his ex-girlfriend, Holly Maddux, and stuffed her body in a trunk which he stored in his West Philadelphia apartment. I was surprised and not surprised, having always sensed something unpleasant about him, although even today I don't know exactly what. He avoided capture for many years and, after some convoluted legal square-dancing, was shipped state-side from France to face judgment. In one memorable last attempt at prestidigitation he tried to persuade the court that CIA agents had killed Maddux in order to discredit him.

Moonlit Tours explores a world where people do not choose evil; they fail to choose righteousness – where the great crimes of life are committed by unexceptional people, people essentially like us.

CREATIVITY

Mediocre art misrepresents reality; great art obliterates it.

The fundamental responsibility of art is to facilitate prison breaks.

Creativity cannot be fathomed, analyzed, quantified, or taught; indeed, it cannot even be survived.

When You Meet Your Demon, Be Gentle

The summer of 1969 found me in McGrath, Alaska, which is only a little further from the moon than it is from Woodstock, New York. I was working for the BLM (Bureau of Land Management) as an EFF (Emergency Fire Fighter), being dropped by helicopters into the middle of active forest fires throughout the state.

Specifically, I was on a back-burning crew, traipsing through dry forests with a flamethrower, fighting oncoming forest fires by depriving them of their fuel. I am glad to report this is the closest I've ever come to war.

McGrath, at the time, was little more than a Government airstrip, some BLM barracks, and a handful of small buildings connected by roughly-assembled boardwalks. The pride of McGrath was a log cabin that served passably as a bar in an area where, with no women to be found, blue-collar men could drink to their satisfaction. A massive moose head, antlers adorned with tinsel, dominated the bar area and the opposing wall featured a full-sized stuffed grizzly bear forbiddingly poised next to the jukebox.

One evening, in-between assignments, I was shooting the breeze with Jake, a fellow EFF. We had money, time, and absolutely no responsibilities – consequently, the phrase about idle hands being the devil's workshop came alive until at last we were drunk; not inebriated, tipsy, three sheets to the wind – not even tight as boiled owls – just good old fashioned, funky monkey drunk.

Jake excused himself to use The Little Firefighters Room and I was left with the moose who, looking even more glassy-eyed than I did, stared with the gloomy insistence so frequently observed among the beheaded.

Long minutes later I heard riotous laughter and watched as Jake lunged and lurched across the sagging floor, collapsing at last on his stool. His balled right hand, clutched tightly in his left, was spewing blood into a rapidly expanding puddle at his feet.

"What happened?" I asked.
"I was washing my hands, you know, and I was staring at the face looking back at me. I mean, it was just so fucking ugly I had to punch it." He laughed extravagantly until tears began to swell in his eyes.

The bartender looked on wordlessly. I walked Jake back to the barracks and dressed his wounds.

CULTURE

America can barely breathe, it is dying of consumption, conspicuous consumption.

White is the new black, silence is the new eloquence, and obscurity is the new fame.

The unexamined life may not be worth living but at least the emptiness is comfy and well dressed.

Chez It Ain't So

Two-time Poet Laureate, Howard Nemerov, and celebrated photographer, Diane Arbus, had a great deal in common. This talented brother and sister act shared what I would call an emotionally brittle nature, and a lifelong battle with depression. Arbus, famously, lost that battle at a young age. Her suicide was no desperate plea for help; she intended to go through with it.

It was 1969; I was a 19-year old freshman punk living la vida loca at Haverford College. My father, Ian, was almost at the zenith of his celebrity, turning up with tiresome regularity in every conceivable media outlet, doing his mad-as-a-March hare environmental activist with a thick Scottish brogue shtick. His base of operations was The Department of Landscape Architecture & Regional Planning at The University of Pennsylvania – a department he founded and chaired for decades.

The Professor was completely devoid of parenting skills, but – having written, and published, my first poem at age 6 – even he knew I was an incipient wordflinger. He taught a course entitled Man & Environment. Do not be misled by the apparent hubris of this title; since he did in fact know everything about everything the all-inclusive subject matter posed no problem. Plus, he invited a long string of tweed-jacket wearing, pipe-smoking, degree-wielding intellectual heavy-hitters to help.

In a rare moment of familial camaraderie, he called to say Nemerov was giving a guest lecture and if I wanted to meet him I should show up at his office about 11:30.

So here we are, three guys in my father's office at the U. of P. Nemerov is pacing and twitching like a crack addict in a rehab. Finally, he says, "Ian, I have **got** to have a martini." My dad, enjoying this opportunity to swagger, tells one of his students to go to the bistro across the street, get a pitcher of martinis, and come back. The student points out that this is illegal and impossible for many reasons and my dad starts screaming at him. The terrified student races away – and is back in minutes with a stainless-steel pitcher sweating chilly droplets. Nemerov's eyes twinkle.

So, I'm thinking – this is pretty cool – I am going to have a martini with one of the nation's greatest poets. As this idea is simmering in my mind – Nemerov puts the pitcher to his lips and slowly, easily, drains the entire thing. My father and I look on in wonder, exchanging stunned glances. I will never forget what happened next. Nemerov stopped pacing, talking, twitching, fidgeting, glancing about erratically, and went perfectly calm. I had never seen a veteran, all-in alcoholic in action before; it was hypnotic.

The three of us walked down the corridor and into the lecture hall. Nemerov read his poetry for an hour; he was note-perfect. I doubt there were more than 50 people in the room, and he was a teacher, giving lectures was his bread and butter. It wasn't about being nervous. Alcoholics get to the point where they need the toxin to be normal.

CYNICISM & SARCASM

Sarcasm is to communication as barbed wire is to freedom.

Cynics: People who have yet to realize how lucky we all are they're not in charge.

Sarcasm, like armor, dazzles at first, grows dull over time, and in the end becomes a mobile prison.

Cynicism: When you're clever enough to see life as it actually is but not emotionally strong enough to accept it.

Earth Day

When I think about Philadelphia's Belmont Plateau on April 22, 1970, I don't think about thousands of stoned hippies basking in the sun, revelling in the nation's first Earth Day. I don't think about Ralph Nader, *Dune* author Frank Herbert, Nobel Prize winning Harvard Biochemist, George Wald, or Senator Ed Muskie.

What I do recall is an enthusiastic set by Native American rock group, Redbone; a bizarre, almost disturbing appearance by Beat Poet legend, Allen Ginsberg; and a characteristically inflammatory performance by my father, Ian McHarg. My dad, let it be said, cut a dashing figure and was at the apex of his popularity. Ginsberg listened to every word like a man entranced. As my father stepped away from the podium, Ginsberg leaped from his chair, wrapped him in a bear hug and planted an ecstatic, heartfelt kiss of appreciation right on his lips.

There, before God and thousands of witnesses, my father lived his worst nightmare. On the one hand, he was receiving adulation from a bona fide legend, and my dad was impressed by celebrity in a way that is, perhaps, unique to celebrities; people who dearly believe in the idea that being known has intrinsic value. So, feigning happiness was mandatory. On the other hand, he was a fearsome individual with a passion for intimidation – war hero, bully, tough guy – homophobia was woven into his tweed. Indeed, he once admitted that, if he had to choose, he would prefer a mentally retarded child to a gay one.

It would be many years before I came to understand that we hate what we fear and build castles of rationalization around our fears to justify the hate. I can only speculate what there was lurking deep in my father's subconscious that nurtured this very particular dread. He was not, as a rule, given to xenophobia; in general, the rich contempt he felt for all humanity was spread equally across its sub-categories. I have also learned, painfully, that such disdain is always predicated on self-hatred.

Ginsberg was almost certainly tripping on LSD that day, his eyes were the size of pie plates and I did not see him blink. Never a handsome man, Mr. Beat Poet was in the full-bearded phase of his career, an entire family of red-winged blackbirds might have broken it up into condos. Overall, he resembled nothing more closely than a member of the underground army, pushing shopping carts by day and snoring in culverts at night.

Unlike the other speakers who, for the most part, were painfully cerebral and sincere to the point of tedium – even for hippies – Ginsberg was whacked. I have never been a fan of the Beats, who damaged American poetry so badly that its battered remains went to die on the lips of rappers; but even a tepid rendition of Howl would have been preferable to twenty minutes of chanting, harmonium squeezing, and casting a flat, vacant gaze into the crowd. I don't think there was any part of my dad's consciousness that could find common ground with that.

At his funeral I made the observation, "Wherever he is, he's probably still trying to wipe that kiss off."

DEATH

Death is not the opposite of life, death is life's twin sister. The opposite of life is cynicism.

There are no guarantees in life, not even death and taxes, especially if you're a corporation.

Not all human sacrifice is equally noble, it depends a little on which human is being sacrificed.

Irony is how the universe tells you to think harder; coincidence is how it knows you aren't.

Dying is easy but comedy is hard. So, cheer up. Even if you fail at comedy you're almost certain to die successfully.

Never Take Advice from A Gargoyle

The dark forces driving mania also drive depression, indeed, mania and depression are like twins separated at birth and raised by different families. The more you understand them the more you are struck by similarities, not differences.

I have written much more about mania than I have about depression, but depression has consumed a far greater portion of my life. The death of my mother, which occurred when I was a grad student, triggered a long down cycle during which being and nothingness seemed almost indistinguishable from one another – it felt as if all color had been drained from the world.

During this bleak season I went on a European vacation with my brother. At one point we joined forces with a Dutch cousin and toodled through France in a borrowed car. Like good tourists we visited Paris and paid homage to the obligatory icons. Climbing the tower at Notre Dame I had an inspired idea for an ad

– Gargoyle with Listerine. After huffing, puffing, and trudging round and round rickety wooden stairs we at last reached the roof and walked into bright sunlight.

Paris lay splayed out at our feet like a pornographic postcard featuring men in masks and black socks held in place with garters. Standing at the edge, no railing to protect us, we gazed at the broad cobblestone square far below; remote and yet close enough so that we were able to make out individual faces. It was a lush summer day, but I went dizzy and cold, sweat grew on my forehead. Abruptly I backed away; the nausea decreased.

It was nothing so simple as fear of heights, or even the proximity of death. The terror was this. If, for just one instant, my inner, irrational mind had taken control it might have moved one foot just far enough to pitch me headfirst into midnight. The faith I had in my mind's reliability – to always act in my best interests – was incomplete. Some part of me knew this was dangerous territory.

Later, in manic episodes, I learned how right I was. Because, dear reader, this is precisely what happens in mania – involuntary, irrational behavior, fabulously self-destructive behavior. Losing control for a second, can mean losing it all.

DEEP THOUGHTS

Anything worth doing is worth doing badly.

How can you think outside of the box when the box is inside your head?

The more you feel you know about, the less you know you feel about, in the dark.

Nothing Recedes Like Success

My father received the National Medal of Arts in September of 1990; other recipients included Jasper Johns, Beverly Sills, Merce Cunningham, Hume Cronyn, and blues legend, B.B. King.

The ceremony took place at The White House, President Bush and wife Barbara (much scarier in person) officiating. Afterwards a select group of 50 or so attendees was invited to stay for lunch (lamb).

I almost didn't make it in. Even though I'd been formally invited my name triggered an alarm when I arrived at the gate because short months prior to the occasion I'd been involuntarily admitted into a state mental hospital.

The White House was much smaller inside than I'd imagined, and I was delighted to find a complete set of Nixon's memoirs in one of the bathrooms.

I had no desire to call attention to myself and didn't want to do anything that might embarrass The Professor; it was his day, after all.

However, at the mix and mingle, right before sitting down to lunch, when I saw B.B. King schmoozing with then Attorney General Richard Thornburg, I simply had to introduce myself. (Frankly I've never been terribly impressed by King as a guitarist, although I do like his voice.)

After chatting amiably for some time, I paused a beat and said, "You know, unlike pretty much everyone else here," with that I swept my arm across the sea of predominately white, male, humorless, Republican, conservative, uptight twits, sycophants, and unctuous opportunists, "I actually own some albums by you."

(This was true; a terrific effort with horns called Blues on Top of Blues and a dreadful 2-album Buddha reissue pairing him with old friend Bobbie "Blue" Bland. In high school I'd purchased an appalling album called Lucille and given it away after listening to it twice.)

I thought this was a slow pitch, an opportunity for us to be amused by the irony together. It is hard to imagine George Bush moanin' about goin' to Memphis to get his hambone boiled, or Barbara cryin' 'cause she need a hot dog for her roll. I doubt that pooling the entire group would have produced more B.B. King albums than Jasper Johns paintings. And yet, nothing at all from The King, just a sour puss indicating I'd given *him* the blues.

Then it dawned on me, when it comes to egomania there is no such thing as success, there is never enough approbation to satisfy the appetite. King was unable to be amused by the irony because he wouldn't be satisfied until the whole world had albums by him. But the bad part is, even then it wouldn't be enough.

I saw this with my father; ultimately the fame meant nothing. As it says in the play Deathtrap, "Nothing recedes like success." And when it does recede, if you've got nothing substantial to fall back on, nothing in the center to nourish you, it gets mighty lonely out there.

Everybody wants to know, why I sing the blues, I've been around a long time, and I've really paid my blues.

EDUCATION

Those who can't do, teach; those who can't teach, teach anyway.

The main difference between changing a mind and changing a diaper is that changing a diaper is possible.

Where you go to college is unimportant, but where you go to high school is crucial, because they will never let you leave.

A Life of Crime Begins Inauspiciously

I have failed in many ways, which helps explain my success. One of the most notable is crime. I'm not exactly certain which element of the criminal character I lack, perhaps if I'd thought about it first I could have studied. Certainly, I have the sloth, entitlement, lack of ambition, and contempt for authority needed to excel, but for some reason life on the wrong side of the law never worked out for me.

Like many before me I dabbled in drug smuggling, which seems ideally suited to unimaginative slackers. A brief, and ill-fated, career began in Izmir, a Turkish city on the Mediterranean. My traveling companion and I secured a kilogram of hashish, neatly wrapped in transparent wax paper and ready to travel. We were on our way back into Greece.

Drug buys tend to be anxiety-ridden events, especially when they involve strangers; being in a foreign country just made it that much worse. So, we were naturally relieved after the exchange was complete to be on our way back up the coast. Giddy with the elation of "getting away with it" we purchased a bottle of unbelievably nasty wine from a roadside vendor. Our route to Athens was a winding road that hugged the seashore and offered spectacular views as it did.

The two of us relished our gangster lifestyle, smoking hash, drinking wine, and enjoying the scenery. It got dark and we discussed pulling over for a while but, with signature manic intensity, I insisted on going until we were back in Athens where I believed we would be safer. We continued, my buddy drifted off to sleep and I struggled to keep my eyelids from drooping. Black night, black sea, no sound or lights to poke me awake, only the waving pair of parallel white lines.

Blubadubablubadubadub. The car was at rest in the furrows of a ploughed field. We checked to see if it still moved and it did. We checked ourselves for cuts and broken bones; there were none. And so, we finally went to sleep properly, it seemed like the thing to do.

The next morning, I scanned the scene with a cold eye. We were only a few feet off the road. On the other side was a long, sheer drop to the sea, certainly 70 feet. I watched as waves slapped the stony beach and realized – this was only the toss of a coin. My stomach tightened like a fist, I fell to my knees right in the middle of the road and kissed the pavement.

EMPATHY

I saw a man with no feet and pitied him until I met a man with feet, socks, and shoes; but no desire to dance.

Before you criticize a man, walk half a mile in his shoes, turn around, retrace your steps, and return them to him.

If your efforts have assuaged the suffering of just one road-weary, hopeless individual, you probably aren't trying very hard.

Ride It to The End of The Line

There's a certain kind of desolation one can only experience by being stranded in a train station at three a.m. An opulent, silent gloom covers every surface like a thin film of invisible grit. The odd, incidental sound, heel scrape, cough, rides a hollow echo and affects grandeur. Night crawlers are all that remains of humanity, pimps, pickpockets, and pushers. The trains are done arriving until morning; even the newsstand is closed. You crave sleep almost as much as you fear it, unwilling to slack off vigilance for even an instant.

It is a form of loneliness, isolation, and vulnerability that seems almost charming in comparison to what I'm after here, romantic and quaint. Because I am talking about a station beyond where the tracks end. It does not appear on any timetable or tourist map. You don't buy a ticket; it's purchased for you, in Bedlam, or on shooting expeditions.

Amidst the rusting tracks and weeds is a station for those who would go as far as they possibly can, at all cost. Where life is not that good, and death is not that bad. Where escape masquerades as fun, oblivion passes itself off as insight, and no monster is more horrifying than a mirror. Where feeling good and feeling nothing are identical twins. A million different paths go to just one destination, and it is always the same.

No one intends to visit this place, it doesn't lead anywhere else, there are no connecting trains. It's an unintended, accidental journey, with an innocent start. For me, a battered yellow school bus winding down the Khyber Pass, leaving the cool, dry mountain air for the humid plains of Pakistan. Bags unpacked in yet another miserable hotel; this time it's Peshawar. Walking choked streets, blazing color, riotous noise. Ascending the smooth, woozy, wooden staircase after spotting the identifying cobra painted on the door. Bald, black midget sporting huge, hoop earring. Money changing hands. Long pipe, black tar, teasing it against the candle flame then smearing it to go, thick taste, almost instantaneous delivery, midget laughing hard at me, I am laughing too, I think, street noise like a blessed magic symphony of blurring swirling nothingness.

A million different paths lead to just one destination, and it is always the same.

ENLIGHTENMENT

Uncertainty is all we can rely on.

Until you've had nothing at all you haven't yet had everything.

Live as if you'll be forgotten only for your deeds, not for your words.

The only road to Heaven runs straight through downtown Hell; and the rest areas leave much to be desired.

Even Hep Cats Get the Blues

My parents met at a dance for foreign students in
Boston. (He was Scottish; she was Dutch.) My
mother, who listened almost exclusively to classical
music and played the cello, would later confess that,
after watching my father perform his rousing Fats
Waller impression she wondered if he might be mad.
(Only later would she realize the complete accuracy of
this hypothesis.)

My father's love for jazz can be traced back to his
childhood in Glasgow where he saved ha'pennies in
order to afford 78rpm recordings by Count Basie,
Duke Ellington, and other American greats. The music
seemed wildly exotic and wonderful to him; moving to
the States post-war increased his devotion.

As a child I was immersed in the exquisite creations of
Satchmo, Billie Holiday, Sidney Bechet, Coleman
Hawkins, Ben Webster and others long before The
British Invasion. (Every so often my father would

regale us with his impression of Coleman Hawkins playing "Body & Soul". This hilarious homage was delivered using only his lips and included elaborate mugging.)

High school and college were devoted to rock; Hendrix had propelled it to the stars. But by the time I got to graduate school Hendrix was dead and rock was very much in decline. I returned to jazz and found that, while rock does one thing very well, jazz is a complete art form that encompasses all elements of the human spirit. Jazz is not so much a musical style as it is a world.

One of my absolute favorite players was a one-man three-ring circus named Rahsaan Roland Kirk. Kirk was blind and famous for playing as many as three saxophones simultaneously. But this only scratches the surface. He would sing and talk while playing the flute and randomly launched into "raps" ranging from political to educational, with stops at race, humor, and bawdiness along the way. Kirk was not easy, but the very definition of a creative genius who could hold his own with John Coltrane, Charlie Parker – anyone!

I saw Kirk perform three times, once at Carnegie Hall, once in a horrid meeting room in Chicago, and once in a tiny Dayton jazz club called Gilly's. I went there alone and got a seat all the way up front. To my amazement, Kirk came into the room from the back and started working the crowd. He was dressed in an orange jumpsuit covered with hooks and zippers and looked like a human Christmas tree except that instead of ornaments there were saxophones, flutes, whistles, sirens, miscellaneous percussion instruments, etc.

He moved with confidence a sighted person wouldn't have had, Kirk knew every stick of furniture in that room, and he sensed every person. At last he arrived at the front of the room, by the stage, next to my table.

"How you doin' man?" He faced me and seemed to know I was alone.
"Great," I answered too eagerly, "I'm really happy about being here."
"I ain't."
"What do you mean?" This confession did not conform to my expectations of the evening. I had been counting the days; some idiot part of me believed that Kirk had also been looking forward to it.
"I ain't feeling it, man. It's Sunday night, I'd rather be at home watching Mary Tyler Moore."
"Why would you be doing that when you could be here turning these folks on to your fabulous music?"
"Because, man, just because. I'd rather be at home watching Mary Tyler Moore."

It wasn't the idea of a blind man watching TV. It wasn't the idea of the baddest, hippest jazz musician on the scene watching the squarest, whitest show on TV. It was the idea that even the most incendiary genius could be vulnerable and flat like the rest of us.

He did two sets; being a professional, they were absolutely amazing. But even when he dug so deeply into "If I Loved You" that I felt sure the notes had been stored in the basement next to the cases of beer, it was impossible not to picture Mary in Lou's office, crying – and Rahsaan saying, "Love is all around, no need to fake it."

ENTERTAINMENT

Beware the tyranny of entertainment.

Propaganda is to art as prostitution is to mambo lessons, in France.

Making education more entertaining to attract insipid students is like making entertainment more educational in order to discourage people merely seeking fun.

Nocturnal Missions and Disappearing Acts

In 1976 I returned to Philadelphia after three years in Louisville where I worked for a newspaper and got an advanced degree. (I discovered later that an M.A. in creative writing virtually assures unemployability.) My mother had died, my father had taken up with a student of his, and I was well into a prolonged clinical depression. I had no family, no job prospects, and more importantly, no will; so, I got a job as a cab driver.

There was an existential purity to that job; it was sublimely meaningless, which was deeply appealing.

For 12 hours a day, 6 days a week, a river of unimportant people flowed through the back seat of my cab. I can honestly say I didn't care about them at all. Some were beautiful, some were ugly, some were entertaining, some were annoying – it didn't make a difference. They all had one thing in common, the only important thing; they needed to go somewhere, and they were willing to give me money if I took them.

One fine spring morning I was dispatched to a Pennsylvania State Liquor Store where I was to collect a fare and proceed to The Alden Park Manor, a stately red brick apartment complex abutting Fairmount Park. I pulled up to the curb and there, holding a brown paper bag and waiting patiently, was an attractive, middle-aged black woman with a wooden leg. (She was wearing a skirt and no stockings; the device was in plain sight.) Neatly dressed and perhaps a bit too thin to be healthy, she looked road-weary and yet oddly serene.

It was a short drive and conversation was minimal. She leaned forward to pay me and whispered.

"Would you like to come upstairs?"
"I really should be going."
"I'll give you a drink." She wiggled the brown paper bag.
"Thanks a lot, but, I can't drink on the job."
"I'll take off my leg," her voice danced musically, "you can have a look."
"Um. Well. Well. Um." I simply could not think of anything appropriate to say.
"I'll let you touch my stump." Her smile was warm and generous.
"Yeah, I really do have to go."
"I'll pay you, I'll give you $20."
"That's all right, thanks all the same."
"The other drivers like it." This was offered with a whiff of bitterness. She opened the door and got out.

I had been living in depression for a very long time, my own pain had become alpha and omega. For that instant she had forced me out of my prison and into hers. I felt the wreckage, the doom, the longing – the strange hunger that would cause a person to abandon all shame and propriety in order to be fed.

The world is larger than you know, I thought to myself.

EXPECTATIONS

We are always experts at the things we never do.

You can always have everything you want because you get to decide what you want.

Why raise the bridge when you can lower your expectations of the river?

Expect people to disappoint you. When they don't, you'll really have something to be disappointed about.

I Sing Because I'm Happy

I felt as though the air had grown thick; I navigated it laboriously, as one walks through knee-deep water. Sweetness and flavour were gone; colors had faded into a thousand grey variations. I was 26 and thoroughly adrift. In need of employment I followed a path worn smooth by thousands of over-educated lost souls before me, complete immersion in a dead-end, service sector job.

Penn Radio Cab was a poorly managed, independently owned taxi company that prospered by transporting Philadelphia's under-served population throughout its most distressed neighbourhoods. We were not Yellow, parked in front of swish hotels, on our way to the airport, oh no. Our days and nights were spent prowling the forbidding landscapes of North and West Philadelphia.

The management at Penn Radio exploited its drivers mercilessly – 12-hour shifts, 6-days a week, weekends mandatory, no exceptions. Saturdays were okay, but Sundays were useless, no fares, no money. Rolling the desolate, trash-lined streets, awash in post-apocalyptic rubble, cars on cinderblocks, hookers, junkies, cops, and newspaper delivery trucks, we ate donuts, drank coffee, and smoked cigarettes.

Early one Sunday morning in April, gritty city trees in graffiti-smeared planters bravely pushing buds out into the carbon-monoxide, I answered a radio call in North Philly. It was a slim brick row house in a block of identical dwellings distinguished by the presence of bright green Astro-turf on the front steps. Out of the house, moving with precise determination, came a distinguished, buttoned-up black nurse. She got in the cab.

Philadelphia is known for its hospitals, so when she gave me the address of a Baptist Church I was confused. In my innocence I asked her if she was attending church on her way to work. She said no, she worked at the church. More curious still I asked her why a church would need to have a nurse on hand.

She said, "You know, in case somebody gets too happy."

Then it all came back to me, like a giant wave. Being a choirboy at St. Martin's in the Fields, my mom driving me and my friends to the service on Sunday, listening to the live feed on WHAT from The Cornerstone Baptist Church at 33rd & Diamond Streets and how the whole congregation sang with a glorious roar of shout halleluiah amen thank you Lord and we didn't know why the building still stood and even then I ached for that kind of faith, belief, that mad commitment and wondered how it must feel to give yourself up to the divine and surrender and then we would go to the ivy draped gothic Episcopalianism of St. Martin's in the Fields and sing and men in tweed with their women in mink would fall asleep and I thought this can't be what religion is.

And so, I drove the nurse to her church.

FAITH

True confidence is so quiet you can't even hear it; you can only overhear it.

Proving that no two snowflakes are identical is a lot more difficult than believing it.

Once you have earned your own trust, investing in the character of others becomes easy.

How to Manage Bullies

Concern about bullies is trendy today, so much so that Hollywood, (where having an original idea can actually destroy your career), has jumped on the bandwagon with its incredibly annoying "It Gets Better" Campaign. (You and I know that in fact it doesn't get better, indeed, it doesn't change at all. What happens is that you either get used to it or you learn how to master it.)

Bullies are a time-honored personality type. (To be honest, we are all bullies to some degree, or at least, capable of being bullies.) Bullies are instinctively drawn to the weak and defenseless; mentally ill folk always make the list. Left unchecked; bullies morph into monsters, I know. Philly, my home town, is among the nation's deadliest cities, thug violence is commonplace. Indeed, I was once beaten unconscious with lead pipes and left for dead in a snowbank.

Back when I was cab driving, a hard-bitten veteran told me, "There is only one way to deal with a gang of "punks" coming for you. You don't run, you don't talk, and you don't make deals. You figure out which one is the leader and you stick a knife in his face." My own mother, a reasonable and patient individual, once tried to run my father over with a 1956 Pontiac Chieftan (a very large car) simply because she could not endure being bullied any longer.

The confrontation approach may win short-term but always fails long-term for the simple reason that it plays to the bully's area of strength; violent brutality. To defeat the bully, you must understand, and eliminate, your fear of him. When he realizes you will accept a beat-down if you must, the power he holds over you slips in-between his fingers. When he looks into your eyes and sees you looking back, the mean, sadistic thrill he craves is gone. At that point he will go in search of less resistant prey.

That is the joyful power and freedom that come from going toe-to-toe, and not flinching. If that is not enough for you, if you are full of hate and resentment, if you dream of reducing this wretched excuse for a human being to a quivering, pathetic blob of sopping flotsam; then it is time to remove the ruthless sword of humor from its sheath.

When you make it obvious you find the bully pathetic and laughable, he is vanquished. And it's a very reasonable assessment because bullies are the very antithesis of what they appear to be. Coming across mean and rough is merely their way of masking cowardice and self-loathing.

Nothing ever just gets better; what happens is; if you're lucky, **you** get better.

FAME

In the future everyone will be obscure for 15 minutes.

The only authentic way to enjoy success is by remaining indifferent to it.

Celebrity: A state of being where one is not known by a large number of people.

Fred Astaire On Ice

Having an unusual name is downright aggravating if you're the type of person who wants nothing more than to skate through life unnoticed. In Scotland, Alistair is popular (Gaelic for Alexander), but on the unforgiving playgrounds of America it's virtually unknown. I have grown accustomed to spelling it repeatedly, and even providing pronunciation tips. The most successful of these is pointing out that it rhymes with Fred Astaire.

Astaire was known for his elegant, fluid style; gliding through densely populated art deco sets like a bird. In stark contrast, when it comes to dancing, I am two leftover feet. However, growing into a reasonable facsimile of adulthood I too developed a terpsichorean signature – dancing through human relationships without ever touching or connecting. Shark-like, I had to keep moving forward to survive and, also shark-like, I consumed pretty much everything I encountered.

Suffering in the shadow of a larger-than-life father who neutralized anyone reckless enough to compete with him, I aimed low. The atmosphere of fierce, unforgiving intensity and extreme achievement threw a warm, appealing glow onto failure, which beckoned like a welcoming friend.

Understand; I had no appetite for magnificent, fearless failure; far from it. I was drifting towards the quiet desperation Thoreau described as though it was a beach resort.

For many people, life has a rather linear quality. Certainly, there are peaks and valleys; moments of triumph interspersed with difficult, challenging episodes. But overall, life is of one piece; there is a philosophy, a rational context, driving it inexorably forward. That, and only that, is what I longed for, safety in the comfort of reason!

Other lives contain a terrible moment of clarity when, either through the auspices of a transformational event, or a revelation of insight, it becomes clear that the life one craved is not to be.

For me, this moment did not occur at 20 as I sat in a German prison cell after being pinched at the Austrian border with a kilo of Afghani hashish.

Nor did it occur to me at 26 as I lay in a hospital bed with dozens of stitches in my face, having been beaten and left for dead one winter night after roaming the desolate streets of Philadelphia alone on a drunken jag, stewing in depression and rage.

It didn't even dawn on me at 36 when, divorced and penniless, I wondered why I'd been fired from two corporate jobs in just six months.

My inability to face the inevitable fueled astonishing powers of denial. Despite the long succession of catastrophes, I still clung to the precious fantasy of a mediocre, uneventful life where I would be spared the demands of greatness.

In 1989, after a spirited round of fisticuffs with two large police officers who ultimately managed to subdue me, I sat silently as the cruiser approached Norristown State Mental Hospital. At that moment I realized there was no chance of leading a quiet, bland life – and wisdom meant surrendering to the life I was actually living. There was no dancing out of this one.

FREEDOM

The only constant is change; well, that and the resistance to change. So, actually, there are two constants.

Freedom is a word coined long ago just in case the state of being it describes should ever come into existence.

Independence is theoretically possible, provided you've got sufficient support.

Crossing the Stream of Consciousness

For all of us, and when I say "us" I refer, of course, to those who society might describe in terms less than entirely flattering, for example, laughing academy graduates, strange rangers, porridge heads, and of course, followers of Lord Whackadoomious, to cite only the most widely circulated, familiar to schoolchild and senior citizen alike, there comes a time and, speaking from experience I assure you it is a time one remembers as vividly as one remembers one's first blackout, if that's not oxymoronic, when one realizes with clarity, certainty, brevity, and afternoon tea that what is commonly referred to as "mental illness" is no mere passing fancy, no hobby or experiment, no entertaining divertissement or amble through a hedge maze but, rather a way of being, not a lifestyle per se but merely a life or, more properly, truly a life, a complete life, which is to say, one will be doing all the things of life, the stuff, the occupations, the challenges, yes, the disappointments and frustrations as well, as a mentally ill person quite distinct from people who, through no fault of their own, are not mentally ill and must raise families, force themselves through meaningless occupations which they call jobs, without even the slightest smidgen of mental illness to make them interesting, and when one has this epiphany, if I may use such a highfalutin word, when a word as unassuming as "realization" would have served just as handily, there is that sinking feeling one experiences upon dropping car keys down a storm drain, that frozen moment of heightened awareness, like the instant before two steam locomotives, accidentally guided onto the same track, collide head on, colors are more vivid, sounds more intense, even one's sense of smell is heightened, those keys, frozen mid-air, no way to reach them, all is gone, all is certain, the die is cast, the cast has dyed, and as the keys descend through the cast iron grill, smiling a mocking, toothy smile broad as the face of a 58 Buick, the knowledge settles in the pit of your pendulum and you make peace, sweet peace, you let go, sweet release, embracing your reality with a brave little smile as you step off the ferry to tread upon terra infirma.

FUNNY

The better your vision becomes, the harder you laugh.

You must first learn how to walk before you can fly in the ointment.

After three days it's no longer a yard sale, it's just crap on your lawn.

If you cannot see yourself as others do, you will never understand why they are laughing.

Welcome to the Back of the Bus

While purveyors of politically correct thought and speech would deny it to their last disingenuous breath, prejudice is very much alive today. It may be increasingly unfashionable to ridicule and despise the "differently enabled" but it is still open season on whackadoomians.

If you have been diagnosed Bipolar recently and, until now, managed to successfully avoid inclusion in one or more unpopular demographic sub-sets, society is holding a window seat for you, and it's all the way in the back of the bus. Prejudice, and the cruelty that comes with it, is always predicated on fear of the unknown. Trust me, when it comes to the unknown, mental illness is in its own class; third class.

The unholy terrain of mania, with landscapes resembling the nightmare visions of Hieronymus Bosch, is more remote than "wildest" Africa, much less a Cher concert. So, brace yourself – all will fear you, some will try to understand you, those who do try to understand you will fail – a small group will accept you as you are and allow you to teach them.

At first, I was deeply offended when they escorted me to the back of the bus. After a while I came to enjoy it there, I loved my colleagues – the music, humor, food, and camaraderie were so much better. I began to think of my status as a badge of honor. I didn't mind being on the fringe; it suited me.

But what really stuck in my craw was the mountain of disdain, condescension, and dismissiveness society rained on us year after year after year. Remember, if you're nuts, you're nuts for life – in the eyes of those around you, no amount of evolution will ever return you to the sane lane.

A quick illustration. My first manic episode happened at age 20, the remaining two major ones happened in my mid-to-late 30s. I was in therapy for 17-years and faithfully monitored my recovery, which included medication and careful reliance on a support network. I even wrote a bipolar memoir chronicling my horrific battle with the illness and subsequent recovery. But in the eyes of friends, family, employers, etc. – it's like losing your virginity – you cannot un-ring a bell.

Nine years ago, fast approaching my 60th birthday, I initiated a major life change that involved leaving one relationship and beginning another, and leaving my home state of Pennsylvania, where I had spent most of my life, for New Hampshire. I thought about this change very carefully, trying my best to manage it in a way that would minimize any negative impact on those around me. (Bear in mind, it had been nearly 40 years since my first manic episode, and almost 20 years since my last one.)

Almost without exception, it was assumed by "near and dear" that I was "going-off" – making this dramatic decision not in health, but in a return to madness. That, gentle reader, is how much credit I got for decades of responsibility, facing my illness, and doing the right thing.

In the eyes of society, once you are crazy, you will never be un-crazy. Welcome to the back of the bus.

GENIUS

One rarely understands genius, but one always recognizes it.

Genius is lunar, not solar; the light it sheds is reflected, not created.

Truth and How It Got to Be That Way

The truth is, we are born into a world of pain and devote most of our brief existence to satisfying base needs. Over time we are damaged, diminished, and ultimately destroyed. Instead of coexisting peacefully with the earth and each other our best energies are consumed by hatred, fear, violence, greed, and self-destruction.

We abhor truth and love lies. Lies are the air we breathe, the earth we tread, the promises of digital technology. Most are so deeply ingrained we no longer even think of them as lies, indeed, we no longer think at all.

Politicians, priests, and corporate representatives spoon-feed lies to the masses because people want to be lied to; lies win elections, build cathedrals, and sell soap.

This is human nature, and I am not so foolish as to attempt a modification of that. However, I will frame it in a context of recovery, because, for the likes of us, recognizing and facing truth can be a matter of life or death.

Lunatics, wing nuts, and whackos – like me – are incapable of distinguishing fact from fantasy. We don't want to live in an abandoned funhouse full of wavy mirrors misrepresenting reality; we just can't help it. Dipsomaniacs, drug addicts, and adrenaline junkies – like me – are capable of distinguishing what is from what is not, but we steadfastly refuse to try. No one hates truth quite as passionately as we do, and when it comes to lying, well; we are the masters.

Mental health involves a long, arduous process that begins by identifying the truth about yourself. This is followed by a hard look at where you are, where you would like to be, and what it will take to get there. Brutal, often painful, honesty is an absolute requisite for this journey.

For many of us, living a life of constant introspection and ruthless candor is rather like learning a new language. But, we tend to be determined, sometimes obsessive, people and what was once anathema can become a familiar, valued way of life.

Then, we get a horrible surprise. Mental illness and addiction have already marginalized us, we have always lived on the outskirts of town; but our newfound commitment to integrity has put us in a ghetto on the outskirts of the outskirts of town.

GOD

Arguing about God is like screaming about silence.

A knowable God wouldn't be, any more than a square circle would.

People are always finding God in prisons and mental hospitals; but try finding a gift shop.

God is in the details and the Devil's in the details. Evidently there's something important about details.

Psychotics, murderers, and those who claim certain knowledge of God's will, are to be avoided at all cost.

Believe Me When I Tell You I Am Lying

As an advertising copywriter I am adept at making accurate statements in such a way as to allow, even encourage, people to leap towards inaccurate conclusions. As a poet I use words with precision and care until all that remains is emotional truth, expressed with as much elegance and clarity as I can summon. So, the duality of language is familiar to me, it is a sublime tool for concealing as well as revealing.

I was raised on a steady diet of lies, as if they were an essential food group, a staple, never out of season. When this happens, it is not long before lies are no longer recognizable as such, they become facts. This is not quite as dreadful as it sounds, we all believe an astounding variety of preposterous lies and many of them yield beneficial results. However, if you are on the road to recovery lies are not merely impediments, they are mortal enemies determined to eliminate any chance you have.

Learning how to stop lying to others is a stroll in the park in comparison to unlearning the habit of lying to one's self. This is almost impossible to do alone – since you are offender, victim, and instructor all at once – it is much better accomplished with the help of fellow offenders. Your brethren in disingenuous locution will be quick to call you on your twaddle and let you know when, and even why, you are attempting to sell a hot, steaming pile of dung to them, and yourself.

As you become relentless about chasing truth, when you come to crave it like your next breath, life itself shifts on its axis. Suddenly it will seem as if airplanes, balloons, and even dirigibles are held in the clouds by lies alone. Like that small child watching the Emperor, you will want to point and shout. Remember, you have changed but the world has not. You have benefited from merciless self-evaluation and willingness to address your faults, but the world has not. Your modus operandi has changed, but take it from me, truth is just as unpopular as ever.

GOVERNMENT

Democracy guarantees the right to choose the wrong person.

Fool me once, shame on you. Fool me twice, shame on me. Fool me every day and you're ready to run for office.

You can't fool all the people all the time; but why would you even try when they're so eager to do the job for you?

Cry Me A River

Manic Depression (Bipolar Disorder) stormed into my life like Godzilla and left like Santa Claus. Among its many gifts was the ability to cry. Until that time, I had fled this basic human function with resolute determination and was unacquainted with its primal power and beauty.

My parents came from cultures where the open display of emotion was anathema; a grotesque admission of defeat and, even worse, bad manners. Both spent their adolescent years surrounded by the cruel chaos of war, which hardened their already Stoic world-views. Essentially their position was; one is entitled to experience moods but there is no profit in sharing them with others.

I soon discovered that feelings could be hidden under layer upon layer of illusion until they became invisible to all. The spontaneous, involuntary expression of sentiment seemed like the province of simple, unsophisticated people – peasants, blacksmiths, hod carriers.

Oddly, I thought of laughter as a cerebral activity and did not yet understand it as the mirror image of weeping. On some deep level I feared that, once crying began it could never be stopped. Being completely estranged from my own inner life led me to wonder if I had any feelings at all.

Mania cracked me open like a cheap piñata at a child's birthday party and before long bats covered the landscape. Fear, rage, resentment, envy, shame; it was undeniable and overwhelming.

In time I learned that mania overrules filters, controls, governors – manic behavior is involuntary. One sees and feels one's true emotional landscape with vivid clarity, whether you want to or not. In mania, and intense depression, one's nerves and feelings are totally exposed; everything is experienced intensely.

How you respond is almost unimportant, what *is* important is that you are unable to process stimuli successfully. You hit "overload" and stay there. During those first waves of 100% manic intensity I cried in bursts, like tropical storms that appear out of nowhere, rage briefly, and then disappear in a blink.

Never before had I felt such blessed relief, such sweet surrender of control. The pain, at last had a voice – it finally had a chance to speak. I listened.

GROWTH

A wall is just a prison cell that isn't finished yet.

If you're the best in town at what you do; move.

It is crucial for the artist to learn their craft; the sooner they do, the sooner they can forget it, and remember their audience.

Shame on You

The earliest phases of recovery are characterized by denial; you try to distance yourself from the mental illness that has wreaked havoc in your life. Gradually you acknowledge the catastrophic messes you've made and claim ownership; your signature is unmistakable. The guilt you experience is not altogether unhealthy as it provides the foundation for action, your determination to not repeat these steps. However, guilt is best consumed in small doses, too much at once can be toxic and counter-productive.

Courage increases as you see the hurt and damage within exposed, perhaps for the first time. The mirror you have finally faced tells an unflattering story, all roads lead back to you, unintentional behavior has blazed a trail of self-destruction and abuse, people and property show the cost of being associated with you.

At this point, shame – that most counter-productive of all emotions – arrives with a custom-fitted iron maiden. The self-loathing begins; you fully understand the source, and consequences – of your illness. You are ashamed of being you.

Right here is where you will lose whatever mojo you once had; cool, swagger, confidence will all abandon you. You will see how the illness is hard-wired into your system – body and soul – and come to understand it not as a flaw but a fact.

Work like a demon, shine the light on your miner's helmet, and you will get to know yourself like never before. Then, forgive yourself – really forgive yourself – and the shame does not have a chance. Hide nothing from yourself or anyone else and your beloved cool, swagger, and confidence will return. But now it is different, now you no longer wear them like suits of armor – now they emanate from within.

Eliminate shame and you are free from the curse of caring about the opinion of others.

HAPPINESS

If you want to find your bliss, get yourself some blisters.

Happiness, we are told, is right around the corner; unfortunately, so is the next corner.

If you don't know what you want, how can you be certain that what you have right now isn't it?

Looking for self-worth in someone else's eyes is like trying to breathe with someone else's lungs.

The idea that happiness waits just around the corner is most popular with people who travel endlessly in circles.

My Mistake

Infallible people never have to apologize, why would they? These are the folks of whom it is said, "Been there, done that, has a medal to prove it."

My own father was one of these blessed individuals, and he constantly reasserted his infallibility by mercilessly bludgeoning anyone who disagreed with him. I cannot recall him ever apologizing. Indeed, apologizing is one of many skills he neglected to teach me.

My own pantomime of infallibility, a sort of homage to dad, depended on a careful balance of arrogance, gullible audiences, and tap dancing. Lacking the big guy's prodigious powers of prestidigitation, I could only keep the illusion alive for a while. Fortunately, when cracks began appearing in the shiny veneer – well – new, less discriminating audiences were always waiting.

Worshiping at the altar of perfection, imagining a model of humanity superior to all others, I naturally came to regard apologies as anathema. To apologize was to admit fault, to shine the unforgiving spotlight on a hideous blemish; either deed – or worse – attribute of character.

Then, two things happened.

First, I completely abandoned what I call "the myth of perfection" which I regard as a toxic lie responsible for an almost unimaginable amount of misery. I accepted myself as an imperfect entity.

Next, I came to understand mistakes as essential to the human experience. Edison observed that his latest experiment hadn't failed; he had simply found another way to not do what he was trying to do. Ultimately, I came to realize, the only people who don't make mistakes are the people who don't do anything. (Ironically, this is the biggest mistake of all, since it wastes a life.)

Now, instead of feeling diminished by apologizing, I feel empowered. To apologize is to cease hiding and take ownership of something you have done. It is also to acknowledge the effect one has had on others; it validates them and puts their needs above yours.

Apologizing is yet another skill I learned in the damp basements of AA. I quickly came to the conclusion that it is one of the few activities in life one cannot do too often. If you have made a hurtful mistake, own it, face it, deal with it.

HEALTH

Time is the secret weapon of education. Cramming for a test is pointless, especially if it's a blood test.

I avoid all political discussions because the doctor told me to reduce my daily intake of anger and stupidity.

Laughter is the best medicine; except when it comes to poisonous snakebites, then it's the second-best medicine.

All You Really Need to Have Is Nothing

Madness – and the madness of addiction – will continue to pick your pocket as long as you let them. If you're stubborn – (and so many of us are, preferring to do things our way rather than the easy way, much less the way that results in minimum damage to ourselves and others) – then it is likely you will proceed in your folly until there is nothing left at all. The question is – how high does the pain level have to get before you are willing to ask for help?

Mania and addiction have both pillaged my life like marauding Visigoths. It is astounding how quickly the fruits of one's labors can be destroyed, if one is truly unhinged. I have closed my eyes on a bourgeois Shangri-La only to open them and discover a desolate, tortured landscape…no home, job, family, property, money…zero, the null set, a goose egg.

Absolute zero is terrifying, of course, but it is also exquisitely beautiful – because what you lack in life's comforts you have gained in vision and truth. Your existence has become binary; you consciously make the choice that nearly everybody else makes unconsciously every day – shall I live or end it? Bear in mind that 1 out of every 5 bipolar adults attempts suicide, and succeeds.

If you are fortunate enough to find even a scrap of resolve, you get up off the canvas and wait for the stars and chirping birds to stop circling your head. Then you get back into the game, no matter how damaged and humbled you may be.

Mania completely wiped me out three different times – after a while, even the end of the world isn't the end of the world anymore. One proceeds. As Churchill – whose battles with depression are legendary – reminded his countrymen when the very existence of Britannia was questionable, "Never, never, never, never give up."

The name of the game is resilience.

HISTORY

Renaming the past doesn't change it, but it does make it harder to find.

Those who learn from the mistakes of history are doomed to endure a quest for new, untested ones.

History repeats itself with tedious insistence; mankind seems determined to perfect its imperfections.

History gladly adjusts in accordance with our needs and purposes; as ambitions change so do the facts required to justify them.

Gallows Humor Swings

If you've been blessed/cursed with Manic Depression (Bipolar Disorder) you'll be spending time off the beaten track, in some cases, far off – for example, you might find yourself lying face down in a drainage ditch paralleling the beaten track, being pecked on the head by an irate duck.

At moments like this you can weep and shake your fists at the sky, or you can scratch your head in wonder at the dizzying, diverse smorgasbord of experiences life has set before you, and laugh with bemused disbelief. Both options have merit, but healthy bipolar bears benefit from developing a resilient sense of humor predicated on perspective.

Laughter sheds light on a dark situation, creates distance, and generates power. Indeed, seeing the absurdity and irony of threatening events is a great way to make them less intimidating. Courtrooms, prison cells, mental hospitals, distraught loved ones, and the offices of therapists are not intrinsically funny – however – the most beautiful lotus emerges from the darkest mud.

Becoming better at doing this means developing the ability to find humor in the most unpleasant, disagreeable situations life has to offer, because these will be the moments when it is most desperately needed. This may serve to further estrange you from those who have never strayed onto the shoulder of the beaten track, much less off of it. In these cases, you can pretend your view is not as wide as it is or acknowledge the distinction and let them deal with it.

In a politically correct environment like ours, where the consensus holds that pretending a Komodo dragon is a swan will make it one, there are those who believe Tourette's Syndrome is comedy gold, ripe with satiric potential – and those that believe it is always wrong to make fun of the disabled.

The problem with this, dear reader, is that bipolar bears **are** disabled, we have already learned that, when it comes to comedy, all of life is fair game, especially ourselves. Indeed, we know that being able to see the humor and absurdity in our own pain, our bizarre affliction, is a key ingredient of healing.

IMAGINATION

Reality can only be found in artifice; mere facts simply aren't honest enough.

The greatest gift that thinking ever gave me was the means to learn that thinking would betray me.

Taut logic taught logically dictates that, speaking tautologically, in the final analysis it's all about the final analysis.

Since anything is possible, the only difference between the impossible and the possible is that the impossible is possible while the possible is not impossible, no matter how determined we are to make it so.

(Note: This satirical piece originally appeared in my mental health humor blog, *Funny in the Head.*)

For Many, Madness Can Be Unaffordable

According to a study released recently by the American Association of Associated Americans (AAAA), insanity may soon be out of reach for all but the super-rich, if current trends continue.

Chumley Throckmorton, PR Liaison for AAAA, explained the findings at a recent press event. "America was founded on democratic values," he began, "our constitution guarantees specific freedoms like speech, religion, and the pursuit of happiness. Happiness means different things to different people, but one thing is certain, for many of us it means embracing our inner whackadoomian and smiling shamelessly as the cheese drifts slowly off the cracker.

"If one quality has helped to shape this nation more than any other it is the enthusiastic celebration of personal insanity," he smiled. "Madness was no mere colorful side road of the American experience, oh no, looneytude carved Main Street out of a hostile wilderness, tied the sky with wire, clogged the air with carbon monoxide, and made the racing rivers glisten with mercury. Toxic levels of greed, ambition, and aggression drove a long parade of pathologically disturbed explorers, industrialists, bankers, bookies, assassins, and interior decorators to ravage a utopia of incalculable natural wealth and beauty.

"That didn't just happen," Throckmorton continued, hammering the podium as the word "happen" arrived, "it took vision, the vision of men and women not afraid to make their demented dreams a reality. But today," he looked down, removed his glasses, cleaned them on his assistant's tie, put them back on his face, and proceeded, "all that is in jeopardy.

"The ever-widening gulf between them what got and them what got not is having a chilling effect on insanity which, in the vast majority of cases, has simply become unaffordable. The result is that our once marvellously wild and obstreperous nation of misfits, malcontents, rabble-rousers, gangsters, and entrepreneurs is becoming white bread, drab, listless, and dull. If this continues at its current pace it won't be long before we're indistinguishable from Belgium...or even Switzerland.

"Nationwide, those who do choose to experiment with insanity today are opting out of the glamourous, high-maintenance diseases with force enough to bend rivers and level mountains for disorders that are more annoying than truly pathological. Complaints like triskaidekaphobia, arachnophobia, and phobophobia may qualify as maladies of the mind, but we are kidding ourselves if we think we can build the nation's future on a foundation of triviality."

Throckmorton summed up thusly. "If America hopes to be the nation it was once and frequently claims to be now it must first find a way to make insanity universally affordable. The painful irony here is that now it is only the rich that can afford insanity and, typically, they have absolutely no idea what to do with it."

INSPIRATION

It's always darkest before the movie starts.

Fearing Fate

Fate is a concept that has fallen from fashion; like honor, morality, and manners. We think of fate as akin to voodoo, primitive twaddle embraced by simple, unsophisticated people. Surrounded by our gadgets, the much-loved amulets and totems of today, we imagine ourselves swimming in free will, shaping our very reality as we go, bending life itself to our wishes. This, of course, is fatuous delusion, the product of our misguided belief that technology will cure the human flaws that have dogged our every step for millennia.

In fact, we are well past the master/slave tipping point and it has become impossible for any serious student of modern life to suggest with a straight face that machines serve us; our habits and behaviors have simply become grist for the mill they own and operate.

We are the raw material; they are the plantation owners. Candidly, you will have to search far and wide in our society for anything resembling freedom and free will; as was the case in post-bellum America, "volunteered slavery" results when the terrible face of freedom rears its ugly head, we race back to the comfort of shackles, all of us.

Mental illness introduced me to freedom, real freedom, the freedom one experiences wandering alone in the desert at night, pursued by jackals. It is every bit as terrifying and exhilarating as you think it is. But today, now, I am more interested in fate, that force we imagine we've outgrown.

I suggest that the only people who would deny the existence of fate are those who have never tried to disobey its merciless judgment, those of us who have never tried to swim upstream, those among us who have never put forth the unpopular, contrarian position just because someone needed to do it and no one else, apparently, had the moxie.

Because, friends, you flee fate at your peril; hide from fate and you enter the old testament world, you get smote with a two-by-four.

Let's paraphrase Shakespeare. "In my stars I am above thee; but be not afraid of greatness: some are born great, some achieve greatness, and some are beaten like rented mules and stepchildren until they finally get a little humility, to say nothing of a clue, and start doing what they're supposed to do."

Greatness lurks on both sides of my family tree like a meretricious monster, smiling its disingenuous smile, lying without even saying a word. As a child I did worship it, like other people, but became more conscious of its horrors than its delights, and soon fell into the familiar pattern of fleeing into escape in its myriad forms; drugs, alcohol, mania and depression, indulging hedonistic appetites, the adrenaline rush of reckless thrill seeking, etcetera.

What comes of wrestling with one's fate, hiding from it, denying it, is simple – and recognizable from far away – you see a man losing a war with himself, a man who has become his worst enemy, a man self-administering the death of 1,000 cuts.

In 1990 I wrote the first draft of my bipolar memoir and in the course of doing so had to confront some hideous realities.

First, of course, came the shame and disgrace of being less than, inferior, crazy. Then there was the ragged history of escape into intoxicants. Worse still was a long string of unpalatable attributes, cowardice, arrogance, entitlement, narcissism, and elitism among them.

But, as I slaved to do the impossible, that is, put readers into the unimaginably foreign world of mania, something even more horrible appeared, a quality I'd feared yet always secretly wondered about; greatness.

Once you have done something absolutely new, something clearly impossible, you cannot pretend you haven't. You know. And if you know, and you fail to act on that knowledge, you are far worse than a slacker – you are too much of a coward to be yourself.

We are put here to love one another, to care for one another. When we don't, we defy fate, and the sickness begins. There are a million ways to be great.

At that moment I ceased being a spy, my double life ended. The polar extremes were integrated into one completely imperfect entity. That is my joy today, just one of the many gifts bestowed on me by manic depression.

INTELLECT

Whales and polar bears, yes; but you will never find intellectual sloth on the endangered list.

Those who believe that intelligence alone can cure all ills possess either too little of it or too much.

Thinking you are better than other people simply because you are smarter than they are is proof that you aren't.

The surest predictor of intellectual greatness is and is not the ability to simultaneously hold two contradictory beliefs.

Great Art Is Made by Great People

As a young person I was impressed by virtuoso artists, individuals with Faustian technique. I imagined how it felt to take the stage, whether literal or metaphorical, and simply blow the audience away – dazzle them with something they had never seen, heard, experienced before. I felt then that it was the duty of art to smash through barriers and open-up new worlds. Only technical mastery, I believed, made this possible.

Much, much later I discovered that this mythology was just so much badoogie, a young man's obsession with ego, self-aggrandizement, and hostility – because that desire to blow the audience away was closely related to "killing" and "destroying" as stand-up comedians use these terms - it was all about demonstrating superiority, establishing dominance. More war than art.

I came to understand that technique is merely a starting point – of course one must master the technical aspects of one's trade – but more technique won't compensate for deficits in other key areas. Indeed, many mediocre artists hide behind technique, lots of glitz and razzle-dazzle, but very little content. In short, the missing ingredient is them. They do magic tricks for the audience, they don't share what's real.

Over-emphasis on technique is what magicians call "léger de main" – the artist distracts you from the lack of substance by drawing your eye to something "bright and sparkly" – and you leave the theatre impressed and satisfied. But this is to art as cotton candy is to food. The true role of technique, and the reason why it must be practiced until it is second nature, is to reveal, not call attention to itself. The best writing is transparent, one sees through it to the meaning residing inside.

Many artists achieve technical mastery, but few are brave enough to use it as a tool for self-revelation, openly sharing their personal truth in a way that allows audiences to feel it and benefit from it. For these special, wonderful people, the audience matters more than the performer and technique is simply a tool for doing important work. I do not for a moment want to deny the sheer beauty of a fugue executed exquisitely, a painting that captures light the way a child captures fireflies in a jar, or a poem crafted with such love that the words chime like bells – these achievements have value in their own right.

But technique itself is never the point. The works of art that last, the ones that lift us off our feet, are the ones where craft was used to create a portal through which we gazed another world and having done so were inexorably enriched.

INVENTION

Art is both a magic lantern that reveals the real ugliness of life and our best, perhaps only, means of redeeming it.

Build a better mousetrap and the world will beat a path to your door. Unfortunately, the mice will switch all your street signs.

Technology has democratized the tools of creativity, prompting a tsunami even more cretinous and loathsome than anticipated.

The Lethal Myth of Manic Creativity

It is said that alcoholism is the only disease intent on convincing those who suffer they're not sick. This deception is, of course, only one of alcoholism's many lies, the first of which is that happiness can be purchased and consumed.

There is a parallel, and equally dangerous, bit of twaddle in the world of mental illness. This nonsense runs thusly – I do not want to "become sane" because if I do I will lose my uniqueness, my brilliance, my creativity. That skewed perspective has led to many voyages of self-destruction, some more abbreviated than others.

At first, alcohol does give one a rosy; numb feeling – so it is not hard to understand how people imagine they're not ill but simply having a good time. Likewise, manic episodes carry much with them to provide the illusion of creativity – boundless energy and confidence, bizarre observations and juxtapositions of thoughts, and the feeling of being "directed" or "guided" by unknown agents. But this maelstrom of mad activity rarely withstands the cold scrutiny and deliberation of daylight.

As I am fond of saying, "Art is not produced by healthy people." Well and good, but this does not mean that being sick – whether by natural or artificial means – makes you an artist. (For years I validated my descent into alcoholism and drug abuse by clinging onto the observation that nearly all the artists I admired, especially the writers, were alcoholics.) Being an alcoholic does not make one Faulkner; being an untreated bipolar does not make one Lord Byron.

The irony here is revealed in a very old syndrome – the human desire to possess the rose without confronting the thorn. We reach for alcohol to make us happy when we know in our hearts that happiness involves hard work – it is the by-product of leading a righteous life. We cling to mania because we think of it as a shortcut to the heights of celestial creativity when we know that even the most deranged, brilliant artists achieved their heights the hard way – dedicated labor.

In madness, and in the despair of addiction, we forget ourselves – what emerges cannot be true because even we do not know what is true. The long campaign of self-discovery that leads to mental health will take you to what is true for you and guide you to creativity that matters.

Art is not flash and hyperbole; art is something divine within that you learn to set free as you heal.

INTERNET

On the Internet, all statements are true; including this one.

With all the expertise being volunteered on the Internet, ignorance is rapidly becoming a priceless commodity.

Is the Internet merely a mechanism by which alien life forms can quantify human gullibility and fatuousness?

Powered almost exclusively by recycling trash, the Internet is helping to frame a green, eco-friendly revolution.

Occupy Inner Space

Terrified and utterly defeated I crawled into talk therapy in 1986 and walked away 17 years later. I learned that analysis is like "exploring inner space" – in the same sense that Lewis & Clark fearlessly plunged into an unknown world. A journey like that is almost certain to be filled with loss, sadness, monsters, bloody struggle, pain, death, revelation, rebirth, and joy. Mine was no exception.

This prolonged excavation prompted emotional, spiritual, and intellectual growth. I'm happy to report it also prompted an almost unnerving creative Renaissance which included a poetry anthology, two novels, two memoirs, and wave upon wave of cartoons, aphorisms, reviews, and essays.

Therapy helped me see that the human heart and soul have changed little, if at all, since the earliest recorded time; we are making the same mistakes we've always made. More than ever I believe that, for things to improve, we must look inside – not to outer space but to inner space – as the final frontier.

Just as we are always surprised to find our keys in "the last place we look" – we continue to be surprised by the idea Walt Kelly coined in his comic strip, Pogo – we have met the enemy and he am us. Looking inside for the cause of our woes continues to be an afterthought, at best.

To paraphrase Yeats, "Wine comes in at the lip, love comes in at the eye, and wisdom arrives at the business end of a Louisville Slugger."

It seems that every day I know a little bit less than I did the day before; although I like to think that what I retain is worth having and sharing. Certainly, my years of battling manic depression and substance abuse have taught me much. With a naiveté one would consider touching were one to encounter it in a developmentally challenged child, I have sought to share what I've learned, to heal as well as entertain.

No need to elaborate on how this has worked out for me other than to observe that social ostracism and walking into a buzz saw are not as dissimilar as one might imagine. But this too is a lesson; ultimately the lack of acceptance changes nothing. To be happy one must do what one was put on earth to do.

LEADERSHIP

Leadership: The fine art of following from in front.

Using fear to lead is like watering your garden with ammonia.

Leading effectively is very difficult when you are inside somebody else's pocket.

Existentialists Explore Extreme Tedium

The word "extreme" is overused today; like "awesome" it has been drained of its raw glory by thoughtless abuse. Being manic-depressive – or "bipolar" – I have spent most of my life in extremes, natural habitat of the mad. I chased kicks obsessively, certain I was having fun. But fun, I discovered late in life, occurs when you know who you are and enjoy who you are; you don't find fun somewhere else, you bring it with you. What I actually chased was adrenaline.

We attempt to make mundane activities sound less mundane by applying the word "extreme" to them, for example – "extreme makeover" – not to be confused with "extreme snoring" or "extreme shoe polishing." But the dirty little secret about life in extremes is that over time they blend together and lose their scary, "cool" edge. So many of these adventures are flights away, not towards.

Mental hospitals and prisons are all basically identical, bland food, linoleum, and well-appointed recreational facilities. In retrospect I realized that most, if not all, of my more extreme destinations - Teheran opium den, Rio de Janeiro brothel, Alaskan forest fires, battered urban wastelands of Philadelphia - were essentially the same place. Ultimately it wasn't where I was that mattered so much as what I was doing there, and why.

Whether by design or, as in my case, fate, it is exhilarating to close one's eyes, sail off the edge of a cliff, crash, break into a ragged heap of fragments – and do it all over again when you heal. The thrill is all consuming, and intoxicating. Doing what most people spend their entire life fearing and avoiding accelerates the process of spiritual growth, but, like anything else, there are limits to what it can offer. Crashing one's car into a wall at 100mph twice is not twice as edifying as doing it once.

The shocking revelation about spending a life exclusively in extremes is that it stunts growth and ultimately is, (gasp), boring. The middle lane is not only the safest, it is the most richly complex, challenging, and satisfying; it's where the real action is.

LEGEND

The only thing worse than obsessing over your press clippings is believing the ones you wrote yourself.

In the warm comfort of obscurity, we are all geniuses; in the cold glare of fame our idiocy is suddenly unmistakable.

One for The Money

"Take no prisoners!" That's what legendary singer Billy Paul used to tell his band right before going on stage.

I've been a performer all my life, singer, poet, comedian, lecturer, maniacal street celebrity.

For much of what I laughingly refer to as "my career" I regarded assassins as the apex of professionalism – heartless and methodical, all business, all technique.

Over the years my attitude about performance has transformed, closely tracking my recovery.

At first, I thought of "the act" as a mask I clung onto with white knuckles, until one could not tell where it ended, and my face began.

As I became more comfortable and facile in front of a crowd, moving with glib, almost condescending confidence, I polished the mask until it shone so brightly even the people sitting in the very last row needed sunglasses.

Then something happened, I grew more confident still and suddenly craft and "art" became less fascinating.

I must credit a few very special people for carrying me across the river; by watching these world class artists perform I discovered that craft is only a tool.

Real art, I came to understand, lies in opening up your true self and sharing what you have, whatever it is that makes you special, whatever it is that's unavailable anywhere else.

Lily Tomlin, Richard Pryor, Keith Jarrett, Sarah Vaughan, Sun Ra, and Jimi Hendrix.

When these people left the stage, they didn't take anything with them back to the dressing room, they gave it all. These giants shared one essential quality; fearless generosity.

Craft is just something you internalize until you can forget it altogether and be yourself – cool, relaxed, smile on your face – bathing in the spotlight's unforgiving chill.

LOGIC

I confess my opinion is absolutely without value; then again, that's just my opinion.

To live happily it either is or is not essential that one learns to embrace self-contradictory concepts.

There are two kinds of people, those who believe there are only two kinds of people and those who dislike oversimplification.

Not Wrong, Just Not Right for Everyone

My father leveraged his iconoclastic, condescending personality into an asset; and rode it to celebrity. Only much later did I come to see that he craved approval, even adulation, the way an addict craves narcotics. Like an addict, his hunger was insatiable; the more validation he received the more he needed. Watching in terrified awe, I grew up believing that mass acceptance is highly desirable, and a reliable barometer of value.

He lived in the spotlight; I lived in the shadow. Growing up in the dark taught me to love the cool, quiet of oblivion, where I was safe from the horrors of accomplishment and the judgment that went with it. If I wasn't known to anyone, (the logic went), I couldn't disappoint. The death of a thousand (self-administered) cuts was well underway.

Manic Depression (Bipolar Disorder) stole the anonymity that cloaked me; fits of mania splattered my once secret torment across the front page, I soon became a nasty joke everyone had heard. For years I labored to understand and remedy what madness had revealed – learning to love the real me. In time I came to understand that honesty is the very bedrock of all recovery.

That is precisely when I ceased being a dilettante and began taking myself seriously as an artist. I wrote my bipolar memoir, applying a raw, journalistic methodology some regard as brutal. From then on, the die was cast. In all subsequent creative endeavours truth - in other words – what I understood to be the truth – became my primary concern.

Everything about my life experience is eccentric, and so, as you might expect, I have many unorthodox beliefs and opinions which I share freely. I certainly don't set out to upset or offend, it's merely an unintended consequence.

There is no alternative. I don't expect universal acceptance – honestly, that would almost be a bad sign – I am merely offering freely to all and looking for my audience.

LOVE

A life well lived is the most thoughtful thank you note.

Love isn't always blind, sometimes it's just ignoring you.

Love can only be understood as a verb; as a noun it can only be observed.

Shootout at The I'm Not Okay Corral

Most of us engage in a rather juvenile fantasy that goes, "If I paint by the numbers and keep my nose clean things will work out well for me." We desperately want to believe in a rational, merit-based world, all the while admitting secretly that life metes out misery at random – at least, according to some concept of justice incomprehensible to us – and seems to be as predictable and responsive to bribery as lightning. As a friend of mine likes to say, "What are you pretending not to know?"

Those of us who have crossed that invisible line and wandered the crooked streets of Cookoopantsatopolis can no longer pretend not to know that – at any given moment – it is entirely possible that things will go terribly wrong. For us, the knowledge, and the fear, are always in the foreground and shall remain there until confronted eye to eye.

This, of course, is the greatest fear of them all – because any foe with the power to turn your life completely inside out is a foe worthy of your respect. However, just because it has killed before does not mean it is going to kill you. You can live in fear or you can face the music and dance.

I was forced to have a shootout at the I'm Not Okay Corral and I'm so glad; since that time nothing has had the power to frighten me. It happened when I was writing my bipolar memoir. Every spare minute for an entire year I threw myself back into the one place on earth I was most afraid to go, the memory of my most recent manic episode.

In doing so I was not merely reviewing horribly painful memories, I was running the risk of sparking another episode. I understood this well, but likewise I understood that I simply had to do it if I was to have any chance at all of getting through it and starting down the road to recovery.

This was a life-or-death situation and there was no guarantee of coming out of it in one piece. For the first time in my life I had to be absolutely fearless and unequivocally committed. Importantly, I understood that the wisdom and bravery of this labor in no way guaranteed it would work, and if it failed, I would be dealing with the consequences on my own.

There is purity and beauty to meeting, at last, the adversary you've been avoiding all your life, the demon you've been pretending not to know.

MEDIOCRITY

Popularity is the price paid by performers who consistently deliver mediocrity.

Being average is a very special gift; find awesome in mediocrity. Do not let anyone talk you out of your right to be ordinary.

Going Public

For many years I hid, in order to keep from being discovered and exposed as a fraud. My flaws were not visible; I "passed" for normal and learned to provide the public with a convincing show. (Much later I would learn that the hideous flaws I sought to hide were imaginary, I was, in fact, no worse than the average Bozo.)

Like thousands of lost souls who eventually find themselves in the damp church basements of AA, I avoided intimacy as others avoid influenza. For reasons too dreary and predictable to enumerate, I imagined that – if you truly knew me you would be disappointed and ultimately repulsed – so I saved us both the trouble.

I was like a John le Carré character in deep cover, impersonating a person, blending in, hiding in plain sight. Writer is an ideal occupation in a case of this type; we are a bit like voyeurs and spies anyway.

So, I honed detachment and isolation down to a fine art. This luscious anonymity was ended by the eruption of mania and a subsequent, highly public, battle with manic depression (bipolar disorder). As I struggled back from the rubble that remained of my former life and, brick by brick, rebuilt and built anew – reinventing myself as I did so – I found that I now had a very real, and very dangerous, secret which had the power to wreck my hard-won recovery.

I understood the stigma; I understood how people fear mental illness. Even criminals fear crazy. In Alistair V.2 I guarded information jealously, revealing only what was absolutely required. I shielded my employer and new friends from my past; every day was spent on eggshells. But, after two cataclysmic manic episodes I realized that I had to know, and kill, this hideous monster, and for me, that meant writing a book about it.

Bear in mind, this was 1990; at the time there was no such thing as a bipolar memoir to be found anywhere. ("Call Me Anna" by Patty Duke was as close as the curious reader could get.) I knew that, by writing my memoir, pitching it to agents, and publishing it – going "bare" for all the world to see – I was making myself incredibly vulnerable to ridicule, contempt, marginalization, prejudice, misunderstanding, and worse. But it didn't matter; I had to do it. It was my emancipation, my offering to the afflicted, and my gift to their loved ones.

MENTAL HEALTH

Over-compensating for your insecurities is like building a monument in their honor.

If you really feel the need to be jealous, then you may as well be jealous of yourself.

For the sake of convenience be your own best friend; it's always easy to get in touch with you.

Never underestimate your ability to underestimate others and overestimate your own capabilities.

I Know Why the Alligator Hides

I began writing **Invisible Driving** in 1990 and ultimately self-published it in 2007 – that was 4 literary agents and well over 100 rejection slips ago. I learned there is something harder than surviving Manic Depression, harder even than writing a book about it – that is, *publishing* a book about it. The torrent of abuse and rejection was epic – at times – even comical. (My step-grandmother founded and owned W.W. Norton – a small, prestigious publishing house – even **they** said no!)

The process was at once humbling and character-building. I knew what I had was good, I knew it surpassed the competition, I knew these unimaginative, lazy publishers were the ones missing out. I came to truly "get" that life is not always a meritocracy, and that acceptance does not necessarily flow naturally from quality and hard work. I grew accustomed to the feeling that jazz musicians must experience when they see Kenny G in a Ferrari; a mélange of rage, envy, frustration, mystification, and absolute certainty there is no God.

During this period I began writing poetry again and was having my work routinely published in one of the country's most celebrated – and bizarre – online literary journals – **Exquisite Corpse**. One day a friend said, "Your stuff is really getting good, you should send it to The New Yorker." Against my better judgment I finally did send them one of my favourites. Weeks later I got the obligatory rejection slip. Without a moment's hesitation I turned it over and wrote, "Dear Sirs: I was saddened to learn of your recent loss. Sincerely, Alistair McHarg" and mailed it back to them.

Childish? Perhaps. Passive/aggressive? Most definitely. But let me tell all of you out there – I know why the alligator hides and I know why he needs his hide. If you are mentally ill, you are going to take some abuse, even if you are trying your best to get better. If you are an alcoholic in recovery, don't expect a parade. And if you are a committed artist, you can hope for the best – that's good, even necessary – but plan for the worst and expect it.

Remember that the rain falls equally on the just and unjust; the biggest mistake you can make is looking up at heaven and shaking your fist. The answer to the question "Why me?" is always "Why not?"

MENTAL ILLNESS

If you need mania to be creative, maybe creativity isn't for you.

If you need brain surgery, it's almost always a good idea to involve other people.

Ever noticed that people who claim to be crazy never are, and people who actually are crazy claim to be sane?

Sometimes it seems like the inmates are running the asylum. Then again, would a sane person want that job?

What I find most annoying about self-absorbed narcissists is they don't spend nearly enough time thinking about me.

Time Loves a Hero, Crowds Like a Fall

If you've ever gotten divorced you know that, as soon as it happens your married friends start avoiding you as if the inability to maintain a relationship is some sort of bizarre, highly contagious skin condition. The fate of those fighting serious mental health issues, including addiction, is far worse.

The road leading out of Bedlam seems endlessly challenging, but we trudge it all the same, then, at the finish line, in place of that brass band we expect there is an angry mob. It seems beastly unkind, especially after the hard work, but before you start nursing a grudge understand a few things about who and what you've become and why the new you is bringing out the very worst this wretched refuse has to offer.

The day you went skidding off the road and right into downtown Cuckoopantsatopolis was the day you reminded every straight arrow of your acquaintance that none of us is ever truly safe. Sanity itself, that sine qua non for the bourgeois, mediocre, pointless life ostensibly guaranteed by the Constitution, is as vulnerable as a Fabergé egg. Nobody wants to be reminded of that, and yet, you do.

"But wait," you say, in that adorably naïve tone of voice you apply to questions that illustrate your innocence, "do I not also teach, i.e. show, that by facing down these unholy perils one can evolve spiritually and grow stronger, actually emerging as a better, more morally grounded person in the process?"

Yes, yes you do, Sparky, and this is precisely why that mob is roughly as happy to see you as they were to see Frankenstein.

It is said in the rooms of AA that a pickle can never return to its previous incarnation as a cucumber. While you may be a reformed devil transformed into an angel, one thing is certain, you will never again be just another Bozo on the bus in the eyes of outsiders; the tired, the poor, the slow, the dim.

Fellow insiders know better, they know that all of us are merely Bozos on the bus, but that is another story.

Your very existence says to these apple pie bakers and flag wavers, "My experience is larger than yours, I know terrible truths you dare not admit. Though horribly handicapped I have emerged morally grounded, fearless, strong, and (most upsetting of all) happy." Trust me, they will never forgive you for that.

You have become a teacher, a leader, whether you care to admit it or not. As ever, peace of mind lies in embracing the inevitable, my advice is – learn how to lead by example.

MISTAKES

There is no shame in ignorance; then again, it's no cause for celebration, either.

All generalizations must be scrutinized with ruthless skepticism, except this one.

You learn from *your* mistakes. All you learn from the mistakes of others is how enjoyable it is to watch others make mistakes.

Syngen the Depressed Clown

Years ago, I was traveling from Philly to L.A. on business and found myself seated next to an unremarkable gentleman – mid-40s, clean-shaven, tall, closely-cropped hair, dressed casually but in all regards neat and presentable. One is captive on a plane and I hoped he understood the difference between friendly and intrusive.

Half an hour later this is what I knew about him. He was a clown who went by the name Syngen and made a modest living working birthday parties, fairs, etc. Over the past year he had become involved in a legal contest with a rival clown, Inspector Onions, who he'd accused of stealing his make-up.

Syngen explained to me at some length that every clown develops their unique look, as individual as a fingerprint. For one clown to steal the look of another clown was egregious. At this point he'd produced a very slick portfolio containing dozens of photographs showing him in full clown regalia – his make-up was so absolutely generic I could not imagine anybody stealing it unless the aim was to resemble every other clown in the world.

But, as it turned out, larcenous colleagues provided only the beginning of a sad tale Syngen told with hideous, obligatory persistence worthy of the ancient mariner. The crux of it was as old as time, love gone wrong, a broken heart. It turned out that Mrs. Syngen had been wooed by a juggler and abandoned my traveling companion, leaving only a note. As Syngen began to launch into this part of his story he gradually lost all semblance of composure and soon was crying convulsively, unable to complete a sentence without gasping for breath once or twice between sobs.

I am comfortable with the dark side of humor; but, one has limits. Certainly, there was something deliciously ironic about a clown named Syngen entangled in a copyright dispute with another clown, so shattered by romance on the rocks he could not contain his despondence; yes, but there was also something creepy and disturbing about it – and the flight was long. So, feeling only slightly guilty, I excused myself and found another seat, two rows further back.

For the balance of the trip I watched Syngen make balloon animals which were passed from one person to the next and retained as desired. I suppose he made about fifty before becoming so lightheaded he had to take a nap. Dachshunds, hippopotami, giraffes, alligators, whales – he really was quite remarkable, and I thought to myself, this is a metaphor for life.

A colleague steals your act, a juggler steals your girl – if you're the clown for the job, you don't let it get you. You lace up the inflatable shoes, stick on the red nose, and make your goddamn balloon animals just like any other day. You rock, Syngen.

But the detail I remember most from that trip is what happened after we landed. Row after row of passengers stood up, collected their carry-on articles from the overhead compartments, and gathered themselves for the walk ahead.

The kids, sure, I got that, and the teenagers too. But even the hot shot executives, smart as could be in 3-piece suits with leather attaché cases – they too all had their souvenir, brightly colored balloon animals tucked neatly under their arms, like irreplaceable, collectible artifacts. They looked perfectly preposterous, of course, especially because, without exception, not one of them was smiling.

MORALITY

When presented with a choice, always take the high road, just remember that doing so makes you a much easier target.

Realizing human character will never improve is easy; living every day as if it must, and will, is the challenge of morality.

Those who would do the right thing because it is, conveniently, also the expedient thing, are already morally bankrupt.

Invisible Baggage

When my daughter was born I wanted the safest car available, so I purchased the first of my five Volvos, the only new automobile I've ever owned. Later I discovered the trick of buying high-end Volvos used, right off a lease, thereby scoring a like-new car at half the price.

I cared for my vehicles with a level of obsession only the mentally ill can muster. They were cleaned routinely and kept absolutely empty, indistinguishable from how they'd looked on the showroom floor. These cream puffs were, perhaps, my only material world self-indulgence. One key element of their care regimen involved always, always, making certain the doors were locked.

With a slavish, OCD-esque devotion to meaningless, compulsive routine I invariably checked all four door handles, and often the trunk, to make certain the automatic locks had responded appropriately when prompted. (Of course, they always had, but one can never be too careful when one's cheese has slipped far off one's cracker, no?) I suppose that, after enduring such terror and madness in my manic episodes, I desperately craved mastery over something, even if it was only my car.

Perhaps the sweetest was a burgundy 850, loaded. My then girlfriend, referred to here as Prunella Entwhistle, and I chose to vacation in Nova Scotia. Going by car meant we could travel every mile from Philly in THC-enhanced luxury, styling like sophisticated Sybarites. And so, we did, cruising to the very northernmost tip of Newfoundland in all its raw, desolate beauty. Apart from the slender road there was no evidence of "civilization" whatsoever.

We parked. Before us the chilly North Atlantic stretched away for miles, and there, right in the center of our view, was a massive iceberg not half a mile offshore, glowing with that transcendent blue one sees nowhere else.

The immense silence was softened only by the ambient sound of waves dragging to and fro across the pebble beach, wind, and the occasional call of a solitary gull. We burned yet another J and gazed in a kind of rapture, then got out for a better view of the frozen mountain, floating so peacefully.

Prunella zipped up her jacket. I got out, squeezed the remote door lock, and checked all four handles. Then I rapped on the window of every door with my knuckle to make certain each was up all the way, (I kept the windows so clean it was impossible to tell if they were open or closed.) Prunella watched with disbelief and then blurted out. "What the hell are you doing? Moron; the nearest human being is fifty miles away!"

My father, quite famously, was blissfully unaware of his inner life, but he did get off a good one-liner from time to time. He liked to tell me, "No matter where you go, you take your problems with you."

MOTIVATION

There is nothing to fear except you itself.

That which does not kill me only serves to make me feel like taking a nice little nap.

Why pay to exercise in a gym when you can enjoy an exercise in futility for free whenever you like?

Before you learn to run you learn to walk; before that you learn to fall on your face, crawl, and summon the grit to get up.

No Man Is a Hero to His Valet

Long ago I was employed by a massive corporation in the business of manufacturing fabulously expensive, mediocre products that were virtually obsolete before installation had been finalized. Within this corporation was a department, enigmatically referred to as Human Resources, consisting exclusively of individuals thoroughly unqualified for meaningful employment.

One day, desperately casting about for ways to justify its existence, the HR Department announced Bring Your Daughter to Work Day. With uncharacteristic esprit de corps I chose to participate in this disingenuous exercise. My daughter, let's call her Guadalupe, was eight at the time, and very like me.

At one point my manager; we'll call him Marcello Anchovy, called her into his office. Marcello was a lovely man, painfully sincere, unassuming, and a subscriber to that delicious myth that it is possible, even desirable, to please everyone.

He told her to sit down in his visitor's chair. She did. Looking at her and exuding all the gravitas he could muster Marcello said, "Guadalupe, I just want to tell you that your father is the funniest man I have ever met."

My daughter's legs did not reach the industrial grade carpeting on the floor of his cramped office and she swung her feet back and forth thoughtlessly, contemplating the ubiquitous baseball memorabilia.

Finally, she looked Marcello square in the eye and, with a deadpan expression worthy of Buster Keaton asked, "Get out much?"

NEGATIVITY

Expect the worst and you're unlikely to be disappointed.

How can you cut through the clutter when the clutter goes all the way through?

What a dull, unnerving, and chilly place the world would be if all crayons were white.

In an age where anti-matter matters more and more, anti-heroes matter less and less.

Death of 1000 Cuts

Ages ago I had a girlfriend I've been referring to as Prunella Entwhistle. Indeed, it was so long ago I was not yet sober and still cheerfully diving headfirst into debauchery as one might leap into an empty swimming pool, at night. This was during that blissfully ignorant period in my life when I believed that, as a result of facing down bipolar disorder and defeating it, I had become bulletproof.

By then I'd recovered from several devastating battles with the terrifying illness referred to at the time as manic depression. I had even written a memoir that chronicled my ordeal. Having walked through fire and survived, I bristled with self-satisfied cockiness and swaggered through life like a cowboy breaking in a new pair of jeans.

Prunella and I occupied a modest bungalow and impersonated adults. I had a mediocre job at an unspeakably dull corporation, and Prunella worked as a sales clerk at the gift shop of a prestigious art museum where she devoted her hours to making personal phone calls and stealing earrings. We were all about phun, or what we thought of as phun, and hopping the Oblivion Express. Very dry martinis, fine imported wine, and the wackiest tobacco on the planet; this was the formula and it functioned with awe-inspiring inevitability.

One Friday evening found us merrily ingesting intoxicants, becoming increasingly boisterous as we did. Prunella and I were sitting in the kitchen after dinner (after all, you need food in your stomach if you want to drink as much, and as long, as possible). She looked at me and, with that charmingly demented enthusiasm and confidence that were her signature, said, "You need a haircut. Let me do it."

Every life has critical moments which, like creaky hinges holding massive doors, mark fundamental endings and beginnings. Should I tell you now that Prunella's infectious optimism was almost always groundless, and that she instinctively returned to dark alleys and dead-end streets with a degree of reliability that might have brought envy to the swallows of Capistrano? Shall I tell you now that it is my nature to trust, even in the complete absence of justification?

Mental illness and intoxicants are like two bad kids in the back row at school. Gravity pulls them together and they seem a perfect fit; but it is best to separate them. Mental illness alone spells bad decisions, throw in alcohol and you guarantee stupidity.

The scope of my predicament became clear immediately when Prunella stepped back to admire her handiwork and exploded into hysterical laughter. I was not able to visit my barber for damage control until Tuesday. During the seemingly endless intervening days I assiduously avoided human contact.

PEOPLE

Parents pray their children will take after them and then are appalled when they do.

If you need both hands and both feet to count your dearest friends; don't do it while you're driving.

In the final analysis it's important to remember that uniqueness is about the only thing we all have in common.

True dedication to the challenge of being you greatly increases the odds of beating out all other applicants for the position.

(Note: This satirical piece originally appeared in my mental health humor blog, *Funny in the Head.*)

Intergalactic Insanity

Since slightly before the dawn of time man has set his gaze on the immensity of space and wondered this – given the billions and billions of tiny dots out there, which are probably quite similar to the thing upon which I reside, circling the sun, or other large objects – and knowing what I do of statistical relationships and relationships of probability, which is to say, the likelihood of events – how could I possibly be alone in this universe?

When you really stop and think, isn't it far more likely that somewhere, somehow, on one of these lonesome magma clumps there is a form of life – however humble – striving ever upwards along its agonizingly slow evolutionary rise which, ultimately, will lead, over endless millennia of failed experiments, to something resembling me, and when I say me I do so because we must take as our starting point the assumption that humanity is what they refer to as The Crown of Creation and as such is the standard by which all others are measured, assuming there are others to measure, which we are, because frankly that is the point of this exercise.

So, let us argue that, given an infinite amount of time to do so, and an infinite amount of government funding to squander, not to mention a rugged little spaceship able to withstand asteroid collisions, exploration would inevitably discover life of one sort or another. According to the legions of marginally employed scientists who have time to untangle these hypothetical quandaries, this is a given. Given, perhaps, but their belief sheds no light whatsoever on the presence, or lack, of mental illness among intelligent aliens.

Since roughly one in ten Americans suffers from some sort of mental illness, it is reasonable to assume that at least one out of every ten extra-terrestrials would suffer from some sort of mental health issue, which in itself would not be bad, after all, we cannot allow ourselves to be prejudiced against extra-terrestrials any more than we should allow ourselves to be prejudiced against mental illness at home – however, in the interests of practicality, and practicality must be our watchword here, it is necessary to realize that not every extra-terrestrial intelligent life form in the entire universe is likely to adhere to the blissfully benign standards of peace, dignity, respect, love, understanding, compassion, tolerance, fairness, and justice we subscribe to here on earth.

This is significant since, in a culture or technology more advanced than ours, the behavior of a mentally ill populace, not to mention leaders, could be catastrophic. So, if we consider space travel at all, we must be prepared for close encounters with alien civilizations in evolutionary stages of development far different than ours, with tastes and belief systems differing drastically from those we hold dear. Consequently, it behooves us to understand alien mental illnesses before we encounter them.

Scientists will quickly point out that it is difficult to study the unknown, which is why we will be forced to take the unpopular option of relying on psychics, faith healers, and social media experts. The time to act is now; before we first encounter mentally ill aliens and wonder what sort of treatment might help them; or protect us from them. So, as you gaze out upon the limitless pinpoints of light strewn zig-zaggedly across the squid ink dark expanse of night, consider this; someone who is not all here may not be all there, either.

PERSPECTIVE

Humility: A sweet lesson taught by a sour instructor.

The more I give, the more I have to give. It's annoying. Soon I'll need to rent a warehouse.

Things just aren't what they used to be; even the end of the world isn't the end of the world anymore.

Prunella Entwhistle Visits the Highlands

Many years ago, Prunella Entwhistle and I took a vacation to Scotland, so she could meet the relatives and eat haggis. A dyed-in-the-wool Romantic, Prunella adored art and was an amateur sculptor. Enthusiastic and impulsive by nature, she was given to moments of inspiration infrequently preceded by rational deliberation.

The vacation progressed well, and we crisscrossed the Scottish Highlands in a rented Mini, lodging modestly in tiny towns with names like Auchnagallin, Kearvaig, and Cave of Smoo.

One morning, as we were leaving the latest in a long line of B&Bs, I firmly gripped the handles of our suitcases to take them downstairs for packing into the Mini. Doing so gave me the distinct impression that they did not wish to come along.

Flummoxed and put off in a way unique to people trying to break camp and get going, I raised the bags slowly – they had definitely put on weight. I was then reminded of a nagging suspicion I'd had – and ignored – for days, that either I was becoming weaker or the bags were getting heavier.

Impatient and irritated I opened them up to determine if this was real or some dreadful hallucination. There, carefully wrapped and stashed inside Prunella's sweaters, shirts, and trousers were half-a-dozen large stones, souvenirs of the Highlands. I was horrified, but it was about to get worse.

I also discovered several whiskey bottles filled with water from mountain springs. As I realized I'd been carrying this dead weight up and down stairs for days – and was expected to carry it through various airport terminals – the blood began to rise like mercury in a thermometer.

Later, after I'd vented sufficiently to make continued travel possible, Prunella revealed her "artistic" plan to install a little garden in our Pennsylvania home featuring Scottish rocks and water. I shook my head in quiet disbelief, wishing for a witness to confirm the depths of my suffering.

To live is to accumulate baggage. It pays to have a good look through the contents every now and again; some beliefs, assessments, values, etc. may have outlived their usefulness. As to dragging around somebody *else's* insanity, well, enough is enough.

PHOTOGRAPHY

A picture is worth a thousand lies.

That the camera cannot lie is axiomatic. But digital technology has enabled manufacturers to correct this deficiency.

The camera has ceased to be a tool for documenting reality. You can no longer believe what you see, or even what you don't.

Glad to Be Imperfectly Awful

For reasons we might want to explore another time, I spent over 30 years toiling in the corporate vineyards as an advertising copywriter – an occupation which enjoys a level of social prestige roughly equivalent to that of garbage collector, lawyer, and snake oil salesman – although to be sure – the latter group is begrudgingly afforded a modicum of respect since almost everyone abhors a squeaky snake. I know I do.

Generally speaking; writers are a disreputable lot. They sleep in culverts and subsist on scraps of food left by others in greasy spoon diners on the outskirts of town, frequently showing up for work with three days' worth of stubble, pockets crammed with losing lottery tickets, reeking of bourbon and cheap cigars. The men are even worse!

As a bipolar dipsomaniac with a chronic attitude problem that includes contempt for authority, you can imagine I lost and found and lost employers the way others misplace car keys. Some jobs were submerged deep within the bowels of soulless corporations shamelessly exploiting the witless populace, while others resided in neurosis factories referred to as advertising agencies where paranoia, throat-slitting, and British wardrobes were passed off as creativity.

One commonality of all these dreadful coalmines was the professional category known as "artist" which, in this case, means "graphic designer" which then meant person in charge of taking words, setting them in type, and embedding the result in a breezy assemblage of photographs, colorful shapes, and visual irrelevance thought to aid the sales process we served; striving ever more valiantly to separate the unsuspecting from their treasure.

Artists – graphic designers – are nearly the antithesis of writers. As a rule, they are cheerful women who bring an ideal suite of qualities to their task – wonderful sense of color, design, ebullience, responsibility, method, quiet productivity, and an almost depressingly relentless optimism. Meet Charity Vanderbilt.

Charity Vanderbilt invariably looked as though she had been peeled from the pages of a clothing catalogue. Her attire was not flashy, it was impeccable, precise, tight, ratcheted down with control as rigid as any painting by Piet Mondrian. Just five feet tall dripping wet, (why she insisted on having her height measured after showering I cannot tell you), she had a sing-song, high-pitched voice that seemed better suited to a Warner Brothers cartoon character than a person.

Her distinctive walk consisted of quick, short steps as though a string between her ankles dictated the precise length of every stride.

One day, Charity revealed something I found completely stunning. She said that the gas gauge in her Volvo had broken and she left it that way on purpose because she "enjoyed the mystery and excitement of not knowing if she was about to run out of gas."

I thought of my own life, a cavalcade of catastrophes including prison, mental hospitals, manic depression, alcoholism, divorce, lost jobs, small fortunes washed away with the dirty dishes – I thought of how I was trying to outrun my curse and find order, stability, responsibility – even some peace of mind.

Then I thought of Charity Vanderbilt, whimsically setting a little booby-trap for herself, to make her life a tiny bit disordered, a tiny bit surprising, a tiny bit interesting. In the oddest way, it made me feel sorry for her and grateful to be me; imperfectly awful.

POETRY

All poets are old; poetry eat its young.

Poetry is far too important to be left to the sane.

Without life, poetry itself would be meaningless.

Writing great poetry becomes much easier when you're willing to die for it.

Armchair Activism

After 9/11, President Bush urged a horrified nation to visit Disneyland. This, he explained, would show terrorists that Americans couldn't be deterred from their God-given right to pursue happiness.

Since then, consumerism-as-political-statement has gained widespread acceptance. This notion seems uniquely American, an odd kluge of our actual religion, Capitalism, and Christianity, the religion we talk about and pretend to respect.

The old sales incentive of – "the more you shop the more you save" – has been cleverly adjusted to mean – "the more stuff you buy for yourself the more giant pandas you save" – as lovely a bit of self-serving pretzel logic as you will ever find.

The idea of making social activism a convenient, spectator sport really hit high gear with the ubiquitous acceptance of so-called social networking websites.

Strolling their busy, digital boulevards one is constantly assaulted by the bizarre promise that simply "clicking here" is sufficient to cure [insert social evil]. Though certain that it's facile, cheap, lazy, and too good to be true; we **_just do it_**.

A while back I realized something truly dreadful: people don't **_have_** problems, people **_are_** the problem. We fall in love with technology and believe it will mend, or at least compensate for, our faults – at best all it ever does is echo them.

As a rule, real change is almost always frightening, painful, difficult, and exhausting. I never changed because I wanted to, or because I thought it would make me a better person. All my growth was driven by necessity, because the choice was simple – change or die.

Anyone who believes that one nimble mouse click will save the rain forest can be made to believe pretty much anything.

Rather than pretending to remedy the world's ills, why not work on the tiny corner of it where you actually _can_ make a difference?

POLITICS

Whenever a moral vacuum appears within the populace there is always an individual with no morals eager to fill it.

Politics, often called the art of the possible, is now better described as the science of rendering the possible, impossible.

On the Internet all are equal and speak with the same authority; this has caused experts to question the wisdom of Democracy.

How to Tell a Genius from an Imbecile

If you've ever known any truly stupid people you've undoubtedly noticed that there's something quite disarming and adorable about them.

The genuinely slow don't really want or expect much from life; avoiding the spotlight's glare in favor of simple, repetitive activities which, while certain to bore the likes of us to tears, provide them with endless hours of meaningless, idiotic entertainment.

Indeed, the stupid in our midst almost never cause real trouble unless they are prompted to do so by unscrupulous, manipulative smarties.

As a group, dolts, dummies, and dim-bulbs are quick to acknowledge their limitations and freely admit they have much to be humble about. They are comfortable soliciting help and guidance, which, ironically, demonstrates a highly accurate sense of self and an endearing degree of humility.

The same cannot be said of the highly intelligent who live surrounded by funhouse mirrors exquisitely designed to deny them the sweet comfort – and wisdom – of unsentimental criticism.

Smarty pants are always surprised, and impressed, by their own intelligence and consequently hold it in higher and higher esteem until, at last, they assume themselves to be the final authority in all things and therefore in no need of education.

At this point they delight in making themselves feel larger still by reminding the stupid of how stupid they actually are, and the stupid, being stupid, and agreeable, play along. Thus is the cycle of arrogance and ignorance stoked like a furnace.

Unfortunately, any individual who asserts that he is omniscient has irrefutably demonstrated idiocy and cannot qualify as brilliant.

More to the point, increasing intelligence and wisdom leads irrevocably to increased humility and admission of ignorance until the only possible proof of true brilliance and wisdom would be utter humility which would posit the significance of what one does not know and the insignificance of what one does.

This would mean that only the brilliant man would know and admit how stupid he is, while the man convinced of his own brilliance would not yet be wise enough to be stupid.

POWER

Power without humility is like a car with no brakes being driven by a blind chimpanzee.

According to a recent study, 9 out of 10 doctors agree that political power is a leading cause of deafness.

Power, like water, seeks its own level. No matter how lofty the source it plunges, inevitably, to the depths.

Just Say No to Nihilism

When you spend a life haunting the dark corridors of mental illness, chemical dependency, and art – well – suicide is always near, rather like those bright red fire extinguisher cases with the label that reads, "In Case of Emergency Break Glass."

Losing a long parade of loved ones to this merciless toll taker eliminates the awe, the terror; glamour and lustre retreat. (Notably, many people choose to purchase their suicide on the instalment plan.)

My generation fell in love with a mythology that linked madness (frequently drug-induced), self-destruction, and the complete abandonment of all society held dear. Our special gift back to the culture busily attempting to spoil us was contempt. Our battle cry – sex, drugs, rock & roll – was easily summed up by a single word – hedonism.

(Need I say we had no alternatives to offer? We romanced nihilism like it was going out of style, which, thankfully, it did.)

This atmosphere proved to be an ideal breeding ground for **artistes** who perfected the empty pose, and empty prose, that went along with it. Kerouac and Burroughs were early adapters, Hunter Thompson threw himself into the fray, and today Tom Waits is a living homage.

Even now these icons of hip negativity and gleeful self-destruction are taken seriously, revered by people who should know better.

I am very fortunate to have outlived my cynicism, sarcasm, and nihilism. Today I find negativity lazy, cowardly, and worst of all – dull. Any imbecile can say no – it's a trick we all learn at the age of two.

To be fair, I also have no time for those who turn away from the world's darkness, paint on a photograph smile, and stupidly say yes.

But time is running out, and things certainly aren't getting better. I seek the people who have looked Satan right in the eye and say yes anyway. They are my heroes.

PSYCHOLOGY

Beware of petting a peeve; they bite.

The smaller the pond, the more grandiose the fish.

One is not entitled to disapproval; one must earn it.

Self-Medication

The first time I heard the *t*erm "self-medication" I laughed out loud. In searching for an analogy, one thinks immediately of the old adage – the lawyer who defends himself has a fool for a client. But that's when the stakes are low, going free or going to jail. How about when the stakes are high? Sanity versus insanity? Life versus death?

Jean Paul Sartre, a very clever fellow, used to play Russian roulette because he was bored. Well, self-medication is like playing Russian roulette with one big difference, all the chambers are loaded.

Self-medication – (the term itself is preposterous) – fits nicely into the insufferable arrogance and egotism of mania – as if to say – I can manage this little spot of bother myself with nothing more complicated than some garden-variety drugs. I remember it all too vividly – "throwing gasoline on a fire."

I adored the adrenaline rush of mania, and I tried to "manage it" with marijuana and alcohol – marijuana to knock the sharp edges off the mania and make it smooth and yummy – and alcohol to slow me down and mellow me out to the point where I wasn't constantly irritated by the sheer inanity of the huddled masses and their inability to keep up with me.

It was an inspired strategy except that it wasn't and a brilliant idea except that it almost got me killed – folks – when it comes time for brain surgery you really need to involve others, professionals – people who actually know what they're doing.

The hubris and sense of entitlement one encounters in a person at the pinnacle of mania are astounding but add in the loss of inhibitions and appalling judgment that arise from drunkenness and you have a confident imbecile who thrives on risk-taking and defying authority.

Some people can drink; I'm not three of them.

QUESTIONS

Failing fabulously is as splendid as success; only not trying is tragic.

Beliefs, and smoke detectors, should be tested regularly, for the same reason.

Show Me the Way to Recovery Road

I entered the damp basements of Alcoholics Anonymous many years ago, and found a new, immeasurably superior, way of life. I won't belabor this point, and I certainly won't try to sell it to you. But I will say it worked for me and continues to do so.

Everything about it surprised me, which was annoying, because I don't like surprises; I'm the kind of person who likes to believe he has it all worked out, (especially when he doesn't), which I suppose is part of the reason I ended up there in the first place.

One of the biggest surprises of all was the amount of humor. Indeed, the process of having your perspective adjusted almost always improves your sense of humor.

In AA, feelings of self-pity and uniqueness give way to honesty and sympathy. You can't really do that without seeing yourself as ridiculous and life as funny.

As this crossover begins, you find yourself laughing at stories that "square pegs" would consider macabre – you laugh in recognition, acknowledging terror, relief, and common humanity – confronting what you fled prompts giddiness.

One of the most delightful things about AA meetings is that there is so much life affirming, healing laughter there. Individuals accustomed to playing the victim and getting others to do the heavy lifting for them find all of this very confusing. To get off the bench and into the game you've got to let go of the twaddle. When the going gets tough, the tough get funny.

It can be no shock to my readers that many dipsomaniacs enter "the program" for vehicular reasons. This true tale concerns one of them. To respect his anonymity, we'll call him Azimuth Pinkerton, (although his real name was McKinley Morganfield.)

Azimuth had wrecked his truck while inebriated and had his driver's license suspended for a year. He was a regular member of a very small meeting I attended weekly, so I got to know him well. Azimuth, who installed drywall for a living, was divorced, a devoted dad to his small daughter despite custody issues, and a convicted felon. He had served a good stretch of time for burglary and had re-entered the mainstream at a disadvantage.

In prison, Azimuth had encountered AA where he'd been told in no uncertain terms that – if he truly desired sobriety – he would have to gain it by "***going to any extreme***" – whatever was required.

One evening he revealed to us that – for his first year in sobriety – with no driver's license and no friends or family eager to help – he had a major problem when it came to attending meetings. This is how he solved it.

Every time he was ready to go to a meeting, he stole a different car from his neighborhood. Azimuth was an accomplished thief and these ongoing criminal acts posed no challenge at all. He always returned the cars to their rightful place, unscathed. Out of a sense of respect, and fair play, he never stole the same car two days running.

There are so many moral ambiguities in this story one scarcely knows where to begin. And yet, after thinking about it quite some time, I say – yes. It's your life you're saving, by any and all means necessary.

RECOVERY

Pretending not to know the obvious is
exhausting.

Be nice to your enemies; you just might be one
of them.

No matter how long you nurse a grudge it will
never become healthy.

People Can Be Important

Human beings are social by nature; one true barometer of health is whether or not we build and maintain nourishing relationships predicated on dignity and respect.

Those of us who have spent time in Cookoopantsatopolis understand what it means to be truly isolated from our kind, imprisoned in an irrational, unsafe world of our own. Indeed, there is no loneliness to match the loneliness of the mentally ill. Alcoholism too is an illness of isolation, a lonely avenue of broken glass.

The very earliest phases of recovery involve emerging from a hideous prison of lies and misperceptions, joining with the world of other people at last. At this point it is imperative to trust; for some of us it is the first time we have ever done so.

Sadly, we must acknowledge that our judgment is virtually useless, and the opinions of others are almost certainly superior to those of our own. Gradually we learn how to gauge our own behavior by reading the eyes of others, in this way we become the masters of our own well-being. The opinions of others become important raw material in the process of self-regulation.

Having learned how it feels to be connected to others, to trust them, even depend on them – it can be hard to know when the moment has come to fly, however, if you are lucky, it will. As a child is ready to leave home, so are you ready at some point to become serenely indifferent to the opinions of others.

Everything in this twisted culture of ours will try to persuade you that winning demands being professionally successful, popular, and rich – but one very important measure of your actual health will be how successfully you avoid this idiotic bear trap.

If you can look at yourself in the mirror without blinking and honestly say you are in good faith, making the most of the gifts you've been given, and savoring this sweet short life – you're good to go.

As a recovered, clear-eyed individual, the moment you are influenced by how your efforts are perceived by others is the moment you begin your fall from grace. If they like what you do, that's great, if they don't, that's great too.

RECREATION

Give a man a fish and you have fed him for a day. Teach that man to fish and you have given him a way to hide a drinking problem.

Critical Condition

If a debilitating mental illness like manic depression, schizophrenia, or Republicanism has stolen your ability to make rational decisions – you've gone through a confidence crushing emotional sea change.

For many of us, it can be months, even years, before we regain the ability to observe, analyse, and evaluate the never-ending stream of input with clarity, agility, and unwavering authority.

Today's recovering lunatic must contend with what I shall refer to as moral and emotional relativism and the insufferable twaddle known as political correctness. Anti-intellectualism is the height of fashion; claiming truth affords one as much credibility as being able to prove it. Sparing hurt feelings now takes precedence over honesty.

Fuzzy-headed social engineers would have us believe that everything is awesome, there are no losers, and all it takes to fulfil one's wants and desires is the ability to visualize and wish with a level of naïve sincerity most frequently encountered in the puzzled expressions of unsuccessful prize fighters struggling through the final days of regrettable careers.

Faculties at last back where they belong, shoulders squared, you will gaze upon the rotting remains of what was once, at best, a mediocre culture and wonder – is this bullshit or is it me? At that precise moment, the extent of your recovery will be determined by your ability to say – this is bullshit – with confidence.

Like a muscle gone weak from neglect, the courage required to repudiate social stupidity must be rebuilt.

RESISTANCE

The worst offense a person can ever commit is being right.

Complain: The only thing to do when doing nothing is just too much trouble.

Possession is nine-tenths of the law; unfortunately, it's that remaining ten percent that gets you arrested.

The Constitution has been amended; it now only guarantees your right to pretend that privacy exists.

(Note: This satirical piece originally appeared in my mental health humor blog, *Funny in the Head.*)

Have Yourself A Narcissistic Christmas

Mental illness is no mere fad, fashion, or lifestyle – it is a way of being. Each particular form of mental illness carries with it a vernacular, a unique configuration of specific attributes reflecting the experiential texture of that milieu. Specific mental illnesses have a diverse palette of associations including sights, smells, sounds, tastes, colors, and even musical forms.

Many of the most popular mental illnesses even have their own favorite day. For example, in the expansive realm of compulsive overeaters there is no day to match Thanksgiving, which, all protestations notwithstanding, is a virtual love song to gluttony.

Gamblers, by contrast, live for the arrival of Super Bowl Sunday when even the most risk-averse and timid in our midst throw caution to the wind and bet cash money on the outcome of an event they cannot control and barely understand.

Alcoholics, a notoriously hard to please group, are known to celebrate pedestrian events which go unnoticed by the rest of us, indeed, for them, all of human existence is either worth celebrating with a drink, or worth fleeing by means of a drink.

Even within this context New Year's Eve occupies a very special place for them. Stripped of all religious consequence, New Year's Eve offers no distraction from the business at hand, that is, two-fisted tippling resulting in a scorched synapse policy rendering participants tight as boiled owls, speaking with lords, and ultimately calling for Ralph.

But the relationship between narcissists and Christmas is of another order altogether, this is symbiotic suitability so intense it makes salt and pepper look like distant relatives. If ever there was a holiday predicated on the burning question – What's in it for me? – it's Christmas.

An airborne fat fellow in a red suit circumnavigates the globe in one night, hurling shabby Chinese merchandise down billions and billions of chimneys and yet for all of us, the question is not, how on earth does he do it? The question is not, am I naughty or am I nice? The question is certainly not, do I deserve things, objects, tokens of esteem?

No, the question is, what did he get me? Quickly followed by, that's not what I wanted, I already have one, that's the wrong color, my best friend has a nicer one, and of course – is the receipt still in the box?

From a mentally ill perspective, and frankly, I look at everything from a mentally ill perspective so there's no point in making an exception here, the magic of Christmas goes far beyond its ability to stir up neuroses, dread, resentments, and nearly forgotten nightmares. The strange alchemy, mystery of Christmas is that on one magical night it brings out the inner narcissist in all of us.

But enough about me.

SCIENCE

Making science your God is every bit as crazy as making God your science.

Can science ever reveal why mankind is naïve enough to believe science can answer its great questions?

Scientists using logic to prove God does not exist are like fish using interpretive dance to prove scientists don't exist.

Science offers us one certainty only - theories regarded as immutable laws today will be replaced by even better theories tomorrow.

Science and religion are not rival methods of understanding the universe, they're rival methods of misunderstanding the universe.

Irony Overload

Picture a glorious living room on Christmas Day. Magnificent high ceiling, cozy fire, exquisite tree, vast windows overlooking thick woods. Now imagine it filled with various members of an extended, albeit cattywampus, family, many of whom have not seen each other for a year or more.

Now imagine that any conversation taking place is a tossed-off afterthought; the primary occupation of nearly all inhabitants is smart phone manipulation.

Now, to me, talking on or playing with a phone while in the presence of another person is rude beyond imagination. To be fair, my parents were both from Europe and very opinionated on the subject of manners. As a result, I have an archaic sense of etiquette which, in my opinion, is predicated on self-respect and consideration for others. While I am still appalled by incivility I am no longer surprised to see politesse slip into the mist where it can comfortably join the dodo.

What *does* surprise me is the almost thundering irony. This astonishing device – no longer anything resembling a phone but rather a palm-sized communications network – has apparently robbed us of our ability to simply be – to enjoy the presence of another – savouring stillness, silence, and calm – to listen, and then, having listened and considered – to respond thoughtfully and politely.

In a word, it appears our need to constantly fetch and transmit information has profoundly damaged, if not destroyed, our ability to converse. (Once again, these people are close relatives and have not seen each other for a long time; Christmas in this case is more than a pseudo-religious shindig, it is an important opportunity to revitalize old bonds and forge new ones.)

When I go into an AA meeting the chairman reminds all of us that phones must be turned off. The reason is simple, what we are doing is a matter of life and death and requires absolute concentration. As the adage goes, "Multi-tasking is the art of doing many things badly at the same time."

Our obsession with gadgets has caused us to forget what many of us never went to the trouble of learning in the first place, that is – the most essential element of conversation is listening and if you are thinking about what you will say next after the other person finally shuts up you're not listening, you're treading water.

To simply witness the life of a loved one, to be with them, is a priceless gift that demands elimination of ego, however briefly. Hard to do that with a horrid monster in your pocket, constantly demanding attention.

Is there anybody left who still believes these little machines serve us, or is it now clear to all we serve them?

SELF-AWARENESS

Why wash your face when you can buy a new mirror instead?

One's own flaws are most annoying when possessed by someone else.

We think of the world as a dangerous place and realize too late we are the most dangerous part of it.

Do not be afraid to be yourself, unless you know of someone better qualified for the position.

When we look for responsibility why is it that we almost always save the most likely hiding place for last?

(Note: This satirical piece originally appeared in my mental health humor blog, *Funny in the Head*.)

Let Your Expectations Fall Like Snow

Heard this one already? Three clinically depressed high-jumpers walk into a bar. They lower it.

I'm kidding of course.

Then again, I'm not kidding, (as always), because if there is anything that will help today's mentally ill individual survive the three-ring-circus of psychological torment and emotional Armageddon known by that deceptively sweet euphemism – the holidays – it is lowered expectations.

Why? With every layer of tinsel, every rehashed Christmas chestnut mangled by Beyoncé, every eggnog-infused martini, every promise of no money down and no payments for the first seventeen months, every drug-addled midnight greeter at Walmart scratching his most recent tattoo, every ill-considered photograph at every office party, and every other cliché of Christmas cacophony and tintinnabulation comes the rising tide of truly ho-ho-horrible inevitability – the hopes, the joys, the fears of all the years, reindeer and pain dear – that Grinch-ish thief of all that is merry; expectations.

Those of us who have mucked out a foxhole or two after the elves have returned to their elf-help groups, leaving only ripped wrapping paper and the unnerving sound of gnashing teeth, know only too well that – an expectation is merely a resentment that has been booked in advance.

We watch the lemming-like inevitability of shoppers who resemble nothing more closely than poor Charlie Brown looking far across the yard at the relentlessly malevolent Lucy finger pointing down at the poised and ready football, believing deep within that dim-witted, soft-boiled egg of a head he has that this time it will be different.

Sadly, it never is. Fellow Whackadoomians, examine the terrible trap we must sidestep. Because it is the Santa-bag of expectations we bring with us – not the event itself – that causes our undoing.

Week after week, the entire culture conspires to deceive; is it any wonder we question reality itself and struggle to differentiate between what is, what might be, and what could be if only we had been less naughty and nicer throughout the year?

The entire communications infrastructure, which now extends to gas pumps, checkout lines in supermarkets, phones, rented movies, in short, everything we encounter in our daily lives, stokes the id until it roars like a voracious furnace – wanting, craving, needing, and hungering for a mountain of flashy, splashy, landfill-food made in China and destined for a useful life so short it would inspire pity in a drosophila, before vanishing out the back end of our consumer economy. It all happens in the bat of an eye.

Want to enjoy your holiday? Do some Christmas triage. Ratchet down the level of your expectations to zero and start there.

SOCIETY

I rely on the American public to disappoint me and it never has.

Bear in mind that equality is an ethical concept, not a biological one.

Human might increases exponentially when individuals form a crowd, while average intellect falls in proportion.

(Note: This satirical piece originally appeared in my mental health humor blog, *Funny in the Head.*)

Signs of Approaching Normality

I've been getting my mail in Cookoopantsatopolis for a very long time now, and the fact of the matter is, I like it here. The people are nice, you laugh a lot, it's never boring, and, frankly, you have experiences unavailable elsewhere.

Another thing. My fellow Cookoopantsatopolis-dwellers are special, they have been through astounding trials and voyages which have given them depth, soul, and character. Now, I don't mean to suggest that Cookootoplians are **better** than square white bread eating mayonnaise-loving Johnny and Jane Lunchbuckets; but I wouldn't stop **you** from saying so.

I guess my point, assuming I have one, is that we all must struggle to know who we are, accept who we are, love who we are, and **enjoy** being who we are. This goes double for Cookoolians who have had to endure harsh judgment not merely for what they **do**, but for their very **being**.

As you move through the various levels of recovery, you may begin to identify with "normal" people, you may even start to believe there is something desirable about being one of them. If left unchecked, this slippery slope will dump you on the doorstep of Squaresville, man – in peril of losing your identity altogether.

Don't let this happen to you! Be on the lookout for the seven deadly warning signs of approaching normality.

1.) You're beginning to think you were too hasty in your condemnation of Disneyland and Disneyworld. "Climate-controlled" entertainment now seems oddly appealing; the thought of visiting Chuck E. Cheese no longer fills you with dread and loathing.

2.) You have begun collecting coupons for products you have no intention of purchasing; you just like clipping coupons.

3.) You refuse to see any movie starring Will Smith because you believe that he became dangerously edgy immediately after leaving The Fresh Prince of Bel-Air.

4.) The prospect of wearing white after Labour Day causes you to break out into a cold sweat.

5.) You enjoy saying, "Muffy and I are having bloodies on the veranda" through clenched teeth; even though you don't drink or have a veranda and have never met anyone named Muffy.

6.) You purchase a Hummer with the intention of installing a Jacuzzi in it.

7.) Even though you have no children, you join the PTA simply because it affords you an opportunity to bake.

Beware! Remember – There Is No "Cure" For Normal!

SPIRITUALITY

If you really want to help yourself, serve others.

All emotional torment arises from the inability to extinguish hope.

Share your self, it's the only thing you have to offer that isn't readily available elsewhere.

Self-Actualization

I have learned never to confuse facts and information with knowledge, much less wisdom. In "the information age" there is an endless waterfall of data, but who is there to teach us how we can make sense of it?

Mere information is almost valueless and the glut of information we have today is actually an impediment to healthy living. As ever, balance is the key – and you will never achieve balance in the absence of wisdom.

One can get education from others but wisdom, sadly, must come from within. In general, the important lessons of life arrive on the business end of a 2×4. So, for starters, don't think there are short cuts; the best way to learn is to live. You must have the experiences yourself for them to mean anything.

I think of the process sequentially, so, for want of a better name, let's call it the *Hierarchy of Self-Actualization* – and have a look.

1. *Know Yourself* – Few people attempt this step and most of the ones that do, fail. It requires curiosity, relentless determination, and brutal honesty.

2. *Forgive Yourself* – Only after thoroughly understanding yourself, the good and the bad, is it truly possible to forgive yourself for character flaws and harm done.

3. *Love Yourself* – Do not confuse this with narcissism; it is all about unqualified acceptance, humility, and gratitude. The universe loves you, why disagree?

4. *Enjoy Yourself.* – You can easily spot people that have made it this far, they have absolutely no envy, they can't think of anyone else they would rather be.

5. *Allow Others to Enjoy You Enjoying Being Yourself* – This is the ultimate, it involves you allowing others to enjoy the real you, even if it means suffering their admiration.

The wisdom here is that you will enjoy life, you will have healthy priorities, and you will have purpose. In a situation like this, doing triage on the deluge of useless information clamoring for your attention will be child's play.

SUCCESS

Hunger is when you clean your plate; greed is when you eat your own arm.

Everything and nothing are identical twins; completely unrelated to enough.

It's lonely at the top. Then again, it's lonely at the bottom too, plus, the service is really bad.

(Note: This satirical piece originally appeared in my mental health humor blog, *Funny in the Head.*)

The Etiquette of Revealing Mental Illness

Mental illness is usually not visible to the naked eye, or the private eye for that matter, or even the naked private eye, although, candidly, if you're being followed by a naked private eye he's the one that needs to be concerned about mental illness, not you – but enough about me.

My point, which is moving across the landscape with the alacrity of a Tasmanian sloth, is this: Whackadoomians have the option of keeping their mental state a secret, a mental state secret – if you will – and if you won't, I will, so it works out. This seems like a tremendous relief, and in many ways, it is, after all this is personal information, often awkward, which we might prefer to keep private.

But it is not as simple as that for at least two reasons. First, if our conditions could have direct impact on others, we are honor-bound to reveal relevant details. Next, we most likely will benefit if friends and associates understand our challenges and limitations. (Many of us lose sight of this because we fear judgment, stigma, and ridicule.)

In AA they say, "You're only as sick as your secrets." All of us know, if only intuitively, that secrets are more corrosive than rust. In an ideal world, one reveals vital information about mental illness as soon as reasonably possible. This leaves us with the question – when is the best time to go public with your mental illness?

Of course, the answer varies from one individual to the next and according to the specifics of given situations – but here are some guidelines.

When interacting with authority figures – before the handcuffs go on.

At work – before you are terminated for initiating Naked Wednesdays.

At a party – before you regale guests with tales of intergalactic travel.

At a restaurant – before you order ratatouille with extra rats.

At church – before you stand up and say, "Oh yeah? That's what **you** think!"

In general – *tell them before they figure it out for themselves!*

TECHNOLOGY

If technology makes our lives any more convenient, even breathing will be too much of an effort.

Technology changes but humanity does not. The stakes keep getting higher while the mistakes stay the same.

TV was once exciting. Every new technology shows promise before plummeting to meet the level of its user.

Humans can repair mechanical problems; but machines cannot repair human problems, only manifest them in new forms.

Only one kind of technology can help save the world for humanity; the kind that is able to save the world *from* humanity.

Extreme High School

Mark Zuckerberg believes I have 304 friends, which only goes to show that even brilliant people make idiotic mistakes.

Anyone who has ever had a real friendship knows it is only possible to maintain a small handful at any one time. Friendships are like pets; they require constant care and nourishment to survive. One may have innumerable familiar relationships which could, under the right circumstances, easily be reanimated; but this is something else altogether.

Although I am no expert in these matters, I do know that – To **have** a friend you must **be** a friend. I've also come to understand that friendship is inherently selfless; one person places another person's wants, needs, and desires above their own. (This would help to explain the paucity.)

The ubiquity of Facebook, with its relentless emphasis on intensely superficial social interaction, (where nothing of value is sacrificed), would seem to bring insights about friendship in its wake. While it does, they are perhaps not the ones we would have hoped to see. Indeed, as we bump masks and publish carefully crafted press clippings we wrote ourselves, the unavoidable lesson of Facebook is as follows.

Remember how happy you were to graduate high school, remember the relief you felt? Facebook is here to remind you that the toys have grown more expensive and the jowls are drooping a bit, but social stratification and playground games are more fashionable than ever.

Naturally, I am interested in this fabulously disappointing phenomenon from the perspective of recovery.

People struggling with mental illness are notoriously inept at making and maintaining friendships. Caring for others, self-sacrifice – these are activities of the healthy; the chronically ill tend to be very self-focused. Also, they often attempt to protect themselves with anonymity, by remaining unknown. They believe that – to know them is to loathe them – so they don't give people the chance. Their principle way of handling relationships is by leaving them.

However, as people grow and evolve in recovery they often encounter a very different reason to sever ties with individuals they once thought of as friends. As they learn to share themselves, their lives, their gifts, with others, they may find that enthusiasm often interferes with judgment. They sometimes overlook

questionable motives in people once considered
comrades.

Frequently they fail to remember that, while *they* have
grown, others may not have been so fortunate. They
often find there really wasn't much in common to
begin with. Most important of all, they feel deeply
that, however lamentable it may be, some people are
simply toxic for them; breathing their air makes them
ill and jeopardizes the mental health they struggled so
hard to attain.

At these moments the old tapes will tell them that
politeness demands they continue to nourish these
vestigial friendships. (They will instinctively
perpetuate these cheery illusions, essentially setting
mousetraps in their own house and then crying when
their toes are snapped.) Those tapes must be burned.

In early days, leaving a relationship is often a sign of
sickness; however, as you recover, it can just as
easily be a sign of health.

TIME

Fate is coincidence plus time.

The future – fun place to visit, bad place to live.

My plans to be more spontaneous keep falling through at the last minute.

The future is a fixed, immovable constant while the past is always changing.

No matter how long it's been since the last time, you never forget how to fall off a bicycle.

(Note: This satirical piece originally appeared in my mental health humor blog, *Funny in the Head.*)

Loneliness: Scourge of the Sane

When it comes to mental healthcare, ours is a golden age indeed. Short centuries ago, strange rangers like me would have seen the business end of society's wrath and suffered mightily. Options included being tortured until cured, or dead, whichever came first, being burned at the stake until cured, or dead, whichever came first, stoning, caning, sarcasm, and ostracism to the far-flung hinterlands where jackals stole what little food was available and rendered sleep impossible with their endless howling.

Today, mental health marches across the landscape spreading chuckles, mirth, merriment, guffaws, smirks, chortles, wry smiles, deep appreciation for the little things of life, and bills. Freedom from the bondage of whackadoomiousness ain't free, we know that, but most of us are quick to point out that it's cheap at twice the price – after all, the alternative is intolerable. And so, with global endorsement, lavish funding, and society's imprimatur, one would imagine that mental healthcare is making tremendous gains, and it is, but not uniformly.

According to a panel of scientists at ASPAS (American Society for the Preservation of American Societies) this is because, while sanity is increasing at a brisk clip, insanity is keeping pace, erasing much of the improvement. When asked what in particular was fuelling the "balmy boom" – ASPAS spokesman Meriwether Periwinkle said, "recidivism. Quite simply, today's recovered whackadoomian can have quite a lonely time of it after being granted their official 'Certificate of Sanity' by local officials."

According to Periwinkle, "Newly sane whackadoomians face a double bind. They no longer identify with active whackadoomians since common interests have virtually vanished. Then they look around for sane people to befriend and discover that the pickings are slim. Unlike people passing for sane, whackadoomians that have clawed their way out of extremis can actually tell the difference between mad and just cranky. They quickly discover what most folks never realize...

"Humanity is divided into three groups, the admittedly mad, the mad passing for sane, and the sane – with the last group being statistically insignificant. Seeking out the company of the actually sane, not to be confused with the allegedly sane, becomes a tiresome chore for many of them, and they return to the familiar bonhomie of Whackadoomia.

"The ones who resist this temptation sometimes must go for weeks without the company of another sane person, fortunately they have learned the wonderful trick of being their own favorite company and thus have a nice time of it all the same," said Periwinkle, who smiled quietly to himself.

TRUTH & LIES

The art of deception comes naturally to those who begin with themselves.

The real tragedy of political correctness is that it has given lying a bad name.

Learn to speak the truth; it is helpful to be fluent in a foreign language.

Lies can only come alive when witnessed and believed, in solitude they slowly starve to death.

Wild Turkey

Philadelphia is one of the nation's most important cities, culturally iconic, socially complex, eminently livable. Like other major metropolitan centers, it has a dark side characterized by heartbreaking poverty, despair, and brute violence.

As readers of my 1st novel – *Moonlit Tours* – will recall, I worked as a cabby there way back when. During that time, one of my fellow drivers was robbed and murdered; shot through the back of his head. They found him wrapped around his steering wheel, brains painted onto the windshield.

A year later I was attacked by a gang of punks, beaten in the face with lead pipes, and dumped in a snow bank to die.

I have spent most of my life in urban settings and consequently developed a rather philosophical attitude towards mortality; a city is a place of police cars, ambulances, fire engines, and endless news reports of senseless death described, and illustrated, in lurid detail. One is tempted to sigh and say, "Yes, so it goes."

But that serene, dispassionate indifference left me when I relocated to the country and had to confront wild animals face to face on a daily basis.

Just over eight years ago I moved to a New Hampshire hamlet so small it does not have a stoplight, gas station, or sidewalks. The rallying point of this burg is a tiny post office with an uncertain future. One day I was getting my mail and who should walk in but our Chief of Police. He recognized me immediately and we exchanged pleasantries. Commanding a full-time force of 4 police officers allows him to take a personal approach to his work.

I began to relate the story of Tom, nicknamed "The Tominator" by my wife, who has a flair for such things. Tom is a rogue, wild turkey who, presumably as a result of turkey crimes too terrible to contemplate, has become separated from his tribe and now works alone.

I am accustomed to watching flocks of wild turkeys ambling through the yard, leisurely pecking the ground, but a solo Tom is new. Snood flapping casually, Tom parades up and down the road in front of our house. His arrogance and disdain are such that traffic has grown increasingly deferential – he is now something of a local celebrity.

We reviewed all this in the Post Office, and the Chief confessed that "dealing with Tom" was high on his To Do list. He admitted to having a net at home. Tom, we agreed, was a danger to himself and others, it's just a matter of time, we nodded in unison, Fish & Game had been called.

Tom has not been seen for many days, and I like to imagine he has been captured and relocated to the tourist country of northern New Hampshire where he now resides in a resort for wayward, unruly wild turkeys. I can accept nothing less, because, as a daily visitor who liked to sneak snacks from beneath our bird feeder, he was practically a family member. But this is not where the story ends.

A few days ago, I was driving down a back road and was forced to stop as a large flock of wild turkeys, perhaps twenty, crossed. If you have never seen one of these magnificent animals, which Benjamin Franklin nominated over the bald eagle for title of National Bird, they are amazing. Imagine a blue-collar peacock, stately, slow, immense, with a truly commanding presence.

Absentmindedly I followed each one as it ambled to the other side, wondering about Tom. I noticed a long, cylindrical shaft protruding from the tail feathers of one. At first, I thought it was a random feather refusing to lie down next to the rest, then I realized I was looking at the back half of an arrow. Not a nice, wooden arrow from the colonial era. No, this was a state-of-the-art, fluorescent green missile made of high-performance polymers, bouncing as the turkey walked.

Clearly it was embedded enough to remain, but not enough to mortally injure the unfortunate creature.

I considered trying to remove the dreadful thing but thought better of it. Then we made eye contact and I imagined him saying these words to me.

"What's the matter, moron, never saw anyone shot in the ass before? New in town? This shit happens, buddy. No sense being sentimental about it. I'm wild, can you dig it? That's why they call me a wild turkey. Takes more than a little DuPont plastic in the hands of some half-blind, half-drunk hunter to slow this bad boy down. Now quit staring and piss off."

VIOLENCE

Inside every bully is a coward; dread the weak, not the mighty.

Never bring a knife to a gunfight, unless you plan on making a sandwich when it's done.

The Inevitable Failure of Technology

A few days ago, I was in Salem, Massachusetts. Whenever I visit this charming hamlet I am acutely aware that short centuries ago people like me, (who manifest mental illness in splashy, colorful ways), were subjected to questionable judicial proceedings, found to be practitioners of witchcraft, and summarily executed. When I leave, after a day of enjoyable tourism, I do so with a sense of gratitude that I live in a more enlightened age.

In the climate-controlled splendor of the Peabody Essex Museum I found myself examining a page from an original Gutenberg bible. Now, we will leave the ludicrous, disturbing subject matter of this dense, complex book for another day and focus instead on the descriptive text next to the glass case which read, in part – Johannes Gutenberg – 1395-1468 – Named "Man of the Millennium" by TIME Magazine in recognition of his profoundly significant contribution to world culture.

Naturally my first thought after reading this was –
wow, who knew TIME Magazine was still in business?

While we think of movable type as something related
to literature and philosophy, it is in fact a
technological breakthrough. Let's say, more
engineering than art. As such, it could never qualify as
the most important achievement of the millennium
because it did not improve the soul of man. Indeed,
by putting the bible in the hands of millions upon
millions it may easily be argued that it set human
evolution back several millennia.

For some time, mankind has put its faith in
technology, with catastrophic results. TIME Magazine's
deification of Gutenberg is an excellent example of
this, as is the recent Steve Jobs adulation orgy. Jobs
was flamboyant and had an uncanny gift for
marketing and developing machines that look and
behave the way people want them to look and
behave. But again, the consequence of his
contribution is strictly technological, not spiritual, and
therefore cannot be considered deeply important.

Mankind does not **have** problems; mankind **is** the
problem. If Gutenberg and Jobs have taught us
anything at all they have proven beyond debate that
more communication is not necessarily better
communication and, as ever, the difficulty isn't the
car, it's the loose nut behind the wheel.

WAR

War is useful to anyone eager to disprove evolution.

WWIII is over, remember? It was US against US, and we lost.

There is only one truly effective way to defend yourself against terrorists; stop creating them.

(Note: This satirical piece originally appeared in my mental health humor blog, *Funny in the Head.*)

Dealing with The Loss of Mental Illness

All good things must come to an end, according to the sage of old, but did you know this also applies to bad things? That's right! Here's the shocker; when it comes time to bid a fond adieu to your particular mental health challenge, you may find yourself dragging your heels, gnashing your teeth, dotting your tees, and crossing your eyes.

Ridiculous, you say? Stifling the urge to cough derisive laughter up your sleeve? Well don't let a little counter-intuition embolden you overly; allow me to share a personal vignette for illustrative purposes.

As you know, Bipolar Disorder is my albatross and it ruled and wrecked my landscape like a series of Old Testament plagues. For years, life was defined by my relationship to this demon and I graduated from mere survival to combat to mastery until, at last, it lay in a heap at my feet, vanquished.

(Aficionados will point out that Bipolar Disorder is incurable. While true, I must add that one can reduce it to inconsequence and insignificance so that, for all intents and purposes, it is neutralized.)

When Bipolar Disorder was in full flower it made me zany, newsworthy, and interesting beyond my wildest dreams. This splashy, sensational illness became something like a really bizarre, all-consuming hobby with a huge payoff, if I managed it I got to live. It even provided the subject matter for my first book. There were times I wondered what I did for entertainment before the onset of my "fine madness."

Seventeen years in therapy raced by until, before I knew what hit me, sanity arrived and with it, the challenge of adapting to normal society as an insider. No longer shivering in the rain beneath a tattered blanket, marooned on the outskirts of town, I bravely faced a life of acceptance.

The thought of being ordinary was oddly unnerving. It was then that I experienced the most peculiar sorrow, grieving for the loss of mental illness.

Remarkably the process broke out over the classic 5-phase grief confrontation sequence identified by Kübler-Ross in 1969.

1. **Denial** – I refused to believe that insanity had abandoned me.

2. **Anger** – I was angry about losing my most marketable attribute.

3. **Bargaining** – I furiously crafted disingenuous deals with a deity I did not believe in.

4. **Depression** – I tried to rekindle the illness by immersing myself in experiences with the potential to trigger a relapse.

5. **Acceptance** – Began insisting on being accepted as a sane person and threatened insane reprisals if I was not.

Only by going through this 5-step process in good faith did I come to understand that saying goodbye to insanity can be a good thing; and that sanity can be a lot more messed up than one might imagine.

WEALTH

The distance between none and some is infinitely greater than the distance between some and a lot.

The best things in life aren't free, the worst things in life aren't free, and the cost of mediocrity is hidden.

Never confuse fame with artistic quality, or wealth with value. Society gets what it wants, not what it needs.

In a culture where success and wretched excess are synonymous, having enough is not nearly so difficult as defining enough.

I Am Not A Victim & Life Is No Excuse

When you live your entire life with a mental illness your relationship with the particular nemesis tormenting you goes through a long, evolutionary arc.

At first there is the glorious warm bath known as victim-hood, in which we indulge as long as possible until at last the water turns cold, grimy, and inhospitable. At that moment we must look directly into the pitiless, unflinching eyes of reality's rubber ducky. We fantasize about having ourselves dry-cleaned.

Our lament of how unfair this all is must finally be returned to our children, where it belongs. Fairness, as we have told them so many times, is not of this world. Stuff happens. Deal with it as best you can but please, no whining.

Then we move into the take charge, roll up the sleeves, hardhat, steel-tipped work boots, seriously eccentric psychiatrist, health-care insurance draining phrase we may think of as taking responsibility for our own well-being.

This simple act, by the way, is certain evidence that you have a chance because, the sooner you take ownership of the illness and make solving it your problem the sooner your journey to health begins.

Next is that most wondrous adventure we'll call opening up the bat-cave of your mind and soul to marvel as monsters of the id tell you all you need to know about - how you didn't get to be the way you thought you would – and - why you drove the cul-de-sacs of unconsciousness, which, with the force of destiny - caused you to be the way you be.

This period of unencumbered self-exploration leads inevitably to the man in the mirror phase where a disturbing realization rears its ugly head, the fact is, we are all responsible for our own dilemmas to one extent or another.

Perhaps we put ourselves in situations that triggered episodes. Did we drink ourselves into familiar stew? What about drugs? Did we sail into oblivion voluntarily?

I used to work with a pleasant fellow named Abercrombie Scintilla. Abercrombie worked as an Administrative Assistant which is the name they gave to secretaries back then. (Another HR Department accomplishment.)

To describe Abercrombie as neurotic, obsessive, manic, paranoid, whacked, and nursing resentments the way a mama bear nurses cubs, would be to use words in an effort to characterize him.

One day Abercrombie, whose desk was not ten feet from mine, screamed in full voice, "***Alistair, Alistair, Alistair. You must see this!***" I heard him bolt from his desk and storm into my office. With passion and torment in fever pitch he thrust a tiny object in my face.

"***Look what they've done to the stamps***," he fumed, face red as a beet and dangerously close to exploding.

It quickly became evident that Abercrombie was unaware there had recently been a USPS design modification, and – no fan of change in any of its myriad incarnations – he found this evolutionary baby step tremendously upsetting.

We are powerless over this glorious world, but we do have power over how we respond to it.

WISDOM

The more you learn the less you know for certain, the less you know for certain the more you learn.

Clever is a poor relation of smart and a bitter enemy of wise. The inevitable consequence of knowledge is humility.

Often it is through the process of explaining a concept to others that we come to fully appreciate the depth of our ignorance.

Save Your Self, Share Your Self

One encounters a Whitman's Sampler of humanity in the rooms of AA - "Yale-to-jail" as they say. Early one Sunday morning, new to sobriety, I was sitting in a bitterly cold, dimly lit AA clubhouse with a small flock of fellow dipsomaniacs. Large, heavily tattooed, and dressed in full biker regalia, a woefully inarticulate ex-con unleashed an incomprehensible, though passionate, soliloquy.

After many minutes of wrestling with the language, and losing, he paused, becoming quiet and still. Then, unable to contain his frustration any longer, he blurted out this memorable phrase with clarity and impact, "I just want to be one of God's employees!"

I imagined a man in work clothes, aluminum hardhat and steel-toed boots, arriving at a factory, punching the time clock and awaiting instructions. He has no will at all, he does not know what the day's work order will be, and he doesn't care. His single objective is implementing it to the best of his ability.

Like so many Americans, I am frequently pulled away from the important things of life by the insane mythology that there is a direct link between worthy accomplishment, fame, and material prosperity. Even as I write these words they seem to belong together, but just a cursory look at our culture quickly reveals that fame and prosperity are rarely associated with merit – indeed, they have become goals, not by-products, which is shallow and very sad.

It was in the rooms that I first truly understood that each of us has the capacity to provide something unique, something useful, something that can change a life, even save one. When we look to convert that activity into cash we're already way off the mark. One does it because it's the right thing to do.

As a writer in an age when people don't read, I don't expect to be a household word anytime soon. I'll settle for sweeping the nation, one sidewalk at a time.

WRITING

Write first, decide not to later, edit later still.

I'm looking for someone to ghost-write my upcoming self-help book.

We write to discover who we are, and in the process, become somebody else.

Writing is the easiest part of being a writer; the most difficult part is becoming a writer.

Great stories usually begin right at the intersection of what must be and what could be; after the traffic light fails.

END